ASTRAL PROJECTION

&

SCEPTICAL OCCULTISM

NICK DUTCH

PARANORMAL PUBLISHING

ISBN-13: 978-0615702841
ISBN-10: 0615702848

First Printing, 2012

Printed in the United States of America

Paranormal Publishing, a division of WheelMan Press

1

This essay is for the sceptical occultist. Not the religious occultists, the believer in spirit beings. This is for those who have an inquiring mind and a desire to come closer to the truth and without accepting anyone else doctrinal points on the way. This is not for the new age movement (which has, by its nature, become a religious movement and not one whose primary goal is the search for the truth), but against it, and as such the argument that is set down here is bitterly against any conceptualisation of a hard and fast objective spiritual reality. However, it is still about a phenomena that is associated with the new age movement, a phenomena that seems to happen and can probably be created by anyone who earnestly seeks that particular experience. I am seeking here, to justify why I don't believe in a hard and fast objectively existing spiritual reality (or am sceptical of others beliefs on the subject) and why I feel that it is right to claim that seeking the experiences that are associated with the new age movement is still a valid pursuit and use of one's time.

There are many reasons to be upset with the new age movement, but none of them are to do with the phenomena that the members of the new age movement refer to on a regular basis. The phenomena themselves, or a certain subset of them, seem to happen and are therefore interesting. But, it is to do with, in my opinion, the kind of *thinking* that the new agers, witches, pagans and occultists do and how they chose to express themselves through language, their use of reasoning.

Thus, this essay is about thinking about the phenomena at hand as well as providing some good quality guidance about the nature of a particular phenomenon, which I feel is something that anyone can have, with enough dedication, experience at some point in their lives. Too many claims are made about what can be achieved by supernatural exploration, too many religious views are discussed, too many religious views justified by those claims, and not enough honesty about what can actually be said about any allegedly supernatural phenomena at hand. It appears that arguing about new religions has become much of what the new age movement has become about rather than any intelligent or scientific research into allegedly supernatural phenomena. This is truly painful to anyone who has an interest in finding out what is real or true in the universe at all, be they sceptics, atheists, agnostics or people of faith.

For instance, if all of the things that new agers promise are real and to the degree that they believe that they are real, then we as a species could have cures for all diseases, mass communication at a distance for free, to be able to know of all things with great precision before they happen, have no need for the slow and clunky institutions of science, be able to do the washing and do all manner of household chores without machinery, disinfectants or other cleaning chemicals and be able to feed ourselves and have shelter at no cost. This is obviously a falsehood, but one that many believe to be true despite the fact that experience shows us that it is not. The views and the thinking of vast bodies of people in the new age movement are flawed.

2

So, let's start with discussing people and their views and then move on to the subject of learning how to do astral projection, or should I say,learning to have the experience, but without confessing the existence of the astral body or any spiritual reality. One of the many reasons that I want you to make sure that you think rightly about this phenomena is by way of a basic cockpit check, to make sure that you are going to keep safe intellectually and that you are going to be able to experience the phenomena without fear.

In order to understand the problem, maybe we have to start with an analysis of people. People who consider themselves to be rational are typically not rational (we are humans, and despite out evolutionary path, we haven't got all that far) and have a point of view that they have settled upon as a result of upbringing or life experience, often stopping at a certain age or stage of development, a model of the way that the world seems to work. A great thinker once said that common sense was based upon certain prejudices that were arrived at by the age eighteen. Experience seems to suggest that this could be true. No wonder we haven't got all that far as a species. These prejudices operate in the same manner as any other from of prejudice and is an action against people who have other points of view, and is therefore a basic tribal instinct, an instinct to connect with people that they themselves feel more comfortable with. Most people's concept of what is real, true or trustworthy comes out of them trusting their own point of view and ignoring the application of scientific thought and creative criticism to their own thinking. Those people who are of faith will recognise an analogy from the Great High Priest of a certain religion here! How can we rely upon the views of such a tribal primitives that are the members of our own species? We cannot! An astonishing fact to many people is that whatever exists in the universe continues to exist whether you believe in it or not. Whatever doesn't exist, continues to not exist whether you believe that it does exist or not. Also, whatever properties a thing has, has the same properties whether you believe that it has those properties or not, be they physical properties, spiritual properties, possession of intelligence or not. And whatever properties a thing has, it has those same properties whether you or I understand those properties or not. Facts are facts, and remain so, but we humans, be we "rational" atheists or superstitious, religious believers, scientists, rich or poor, of whatever persuasion or lack of it, are driven by beliefs and not enough doubt to perpetually ask ourselves whether we are or have the capacity to be wrong about something. Something ceases to exist or be real to someone when they stop believing in it, which, by reasoning, we can say is stupidity in the extreme. This is in its own right, a form of mental illness of sorts and a lunacy that we humans have come to perceive as normal in our society and culture as a result of our culturation, the things that help us to integrate socially. But the things that help us to integrate with our fellow human tribal primitives won't help us as a species to learn more about the world that we live in or to explore strange, new, interesting or different phenomena. It is quite an unscientific attitude in a society that believes itself to be rational or advanced to perpetuate this way of thinking and behaving! So unscientific that we might as well call it superstitious.

There was a time in the twentieth century when a certain writer exclaimed that everything in the world had already been invented and suggested that progress could not go an further. This was before the advent of the computer and the silicon chip, thus proving that no matter how far we develop and how much we know, and how much we can invent or achieve, there is ALWAYS more on the horizon. It is only stubbornness of thinking and an unwillingness to investigate further that gets in our way. Cult thinking and certain types of religious thought can obscure our progress like a blurry distorting lens being placed in the path of clear pure light.

How can we keep the arrogant attitude that the beliefs of an apparent elite (those who state to us what is real and what is not) are an expression of what is complete and total facts of the universe? How much is there to find out? What we currently know about life, the Universe and Everything is pathetic by comparison to what there is to know. What we have currently invented and achieved is pathetic by comparison to what we as a species have yet to achieve and invent. Instead of being complacent in our knowledge, lets say instead "Maybe we have it wrong? Maybe we don't know enough? Why should I stop with that perspective on reality? Maybe we just don't currently know? And maybe we can work hard to find out some more!"

There has always been a move to suppress one point of view and to encourage another, instead of to say "we just don't know, but we are willing to find out". It is a human thing. Once it was a religious group that had the power, now it seems that Scientists who worship their intangible god like concept that they call Reason (and I might add, without knowing, in many cases, what it means to be able to reason!) seem to rule the roost, and to make matters worse, the New Age movement is perfectly willing to add more problems to a complex society through ignoring even the most basic of scientific methodology when they talk about their beliefs which they talk about as if they were facts.

The suppression of knowledge is sometimes done

with sound motives, but sometimes it is done with political or ideological reasons that are so far removed from reason as to be primitive in their attitude or indeed may have other dangers. Sometimes some kinds of suppression occurs purely for financial gain or the sick desire to weaken other humans to the point of making them vulnerable. Removing power from one group of maniacs and placing power in the hands of another. We see this in most movements. Exchanging one evil for another.

So, lets change the dialogue. **Let's be honest for a change and say that there are some strange experiences which seem to occur.** Experiences that come about as a result of meditation and religious practices and that are interesting. **But, do they always prove or suggest that which they seem to prove or suggest? No! Naturally, they do not!**

If we were to have listened to the pundit that I have mentioned a few paragraphs ago, air travel wouldn't have advanced much beyond the Wright brothers technology, we would not have computers or the internet, and, by extension, the Arab Spring which was influenced by social media, satellite technology and the internet (products of courageous research into nature), wouldn't have happened and our societies would be even more closed and primitive. If it wasn't for the pioneers of the early days of science who were performing forbidden activities, we would not have modern science. How much more can we achieve as a species of the limitations of dogmatic religion are taking away from research into the paranormal?

So what is this paranormal and the phenomena of astral projection of which I speak and why is it important? It is, in accordance with my own experience and experimentation, an unempirical experiential art form. The word "unempirical" means that it can't be investigated in the same manner as the physical sciences. Experiential means that it is investigated by experience. Art form means that it relies on creative problem solving and the perpetual improvement of skill. Thus understanding the words that we use when discussing this subject is essential. But due to the nature of the phenomena at hand, and the things that it relies upon, namely the body and the mind of a human being, there is always to be some problems with making the phenomena work according to plan or reliably.

It is based on experiences in meditation and religious states of mind. It uses visualisation, suggestion and more. It can, in some rare and extreme cases, give you the same or similar experiences which some prophets, spiritualists and religious sages have used as their justification to believe in Telepathy, Precognition, Prophecy, God, Angels, Life after Death and Spirits. However, it cannot under any circumstances give you any definitive or conclusive proof of the existence of these beings and forces. Seeing those experiences as conclusive proof is shallow reasoning indeed, but very popular in the new age movement.

We have to be perpetually humbled to the idea that these experience which seem to be "paranormal", "occult" or "magickal" things that we experience are just that. Experiences. No matter how strange or unusual these experiences are, no matter how solid and real the spirit beings that we see seem to be, no matter how accurate our prophecies, no matter how reliable our apparently telepathic experiences are, these things are just strange experiences.

EXPERIENCES ONLY PROVE THAT EXPERIENCES CAN HAPPEN.

STRANGE EXPERIENCES DO NOT UNDER ANY CIRCUMSTANCES GIVE YOU PROOF THAT THE THINGS THAT THESE EXPERIENCES SEEM TO SUGGEST ARE REAL.

"PROOF" AND "EVIDENCE" ARE MERELY STAGES IN AN ACADEMIC DEBATE AND ARE SELDOM CONCLUSIVE NO MATTER WHAT SOME PEOPLE SAY.

ANY BELIEFS THAT WE DEVELOP AS A RESULT OF THESE EXPERIENCES ARE BELIEFS AND ARE THEREFORE, AND WE CAN SAY THIS BY REA-

SON AND THOUGHT, DOWNRIGHT WRONG, INNACURATE OR A POOR LOW RESOLUTON OUTLINE OF WHATEVER IS TRUE AT BEST.

ALL BELIEFS ARE JUST A REFLECTION OF OUR ATTEMPT TO UNDERSTAND THE WORLD. THEY ARE NOT FACTS!

The only thing that we can say is that these experiences say something about us as humans as we have the capacity to have these experiences. But what they mean we will probably never know, not in my or your lifetime anyway. What they mean in terms of the way that the universe works, will always remain a mystery.

But, the experiences carry on, people report them world wide. People start to develop new spiritual paths, new religions and new ides based on these experiences. What is wrong on so many levels is the tendency that humans have to view these new beliefs as facts without even going to the level of scientific inquiry to ascertain what is fact and what is not a fact. Its quite disheartening really.

As a result of this, Ufology has become a religion as a product of some people seeing weather balloons, some strange people worship electricity as a god, others call the Bible "fairy stories", but instead believe in faeries. Therefore we can see why members of the new age movement get laughed at.

Anyone can see a ghost, but that doesn't prove that Ghosts exist nor does it prove that there is life after death and it certainly doesn't prove the existence of the astral body. It proves the strange experience is possible to happen. That is all. I can use language to explain the experience by suggesting that it fulfills what our culture would call the experience of seeing a ghost, but one still can't say that the Ghost actually existed. Using the phrase "I saw a ghost" MUST therefore be seen as a way of saying "I had a strange experience which our culture would call 'seeing a ghost' but I have no idea and I can't prove that the ghost existed in any real objective manner, I certainly cant prove that there is life after death and I have no objective evidence apart from the experience, that I saw a 'thing' and that that thing was conscious or had some kind of awareness, nor indeed that it could see me". However, thanks to popular media and the current level of "advancement" of the intellect of our species, the phrase is used to support a religious point of view namely that Ghosts exist objectively and there is life after death. This mustn't carry on especially if we are to research more deeply into these strange experiences to get some clarity on how the world works

3

Consciousness science is incomplete, we as humans know precious little about the universe and even about our own minds. More case studies are needed, more reported strange experiences, more anecdotes. I include a small selection of my own anecdotes further along in this essay for you to use for inspirational purposes and to help you along in your path of learning about this phenomena of Astral Projection. One of the many reasons I am writing this is to motivate you to want to have these experiences and, by extension, to enhance our understanding of the natural world. Our understanding of the world as a species, not just YOUR understanding of beliefs. I am certainly not writing this to help you to believe more in the afterlife.

One day someone will be able to make sense of all of this. Some broad minded group of specialist scientists. But, that is many many centuries in the future, but it will happen (I hope so anyway).

For the moment, seek the strange experiences and have fun (for that's what it is), but remain as sceptical and doubting as is possible. That is the only way to keep your sanity.

And yes I have used the word "sanity" and I feel that I could be classed as being very well advised in doing so. The new age, occult and pagan movements have gone out of control. We don't need even more cults, we don't need any more religions. We just need to think intelligently about what is real and what we have experienced.

It is astonishing to my mind that such a group of people can be so passionate about what they believe, want to strike terror in the hearts of their followers about what their interpretation of spiritualism can do, the alleged powers of entities and so on, but can't maintain a logically consistent argument about their own ideas and instead of choosing to apply some scientific rigour to their views on the way that the natural world works, instead become as bad as any other religious extremist. They do this despite their claims of miraculous healing, telepathy and all the rest being hard and fast facts of the universe and that they alone have the key to unlock its power. Many of them laughingly claim that their occultism the way that they do it and the way that thy think about it is scientific.

Such a way of acting to me is morally abhorrent, and such a way of thinking is intellectually so far in the kindergarten that it is failing at finger painting class.

So, are there beings and energies that one can communicate with using "magick" that are hitherto unresearched by profane science? We cannot say. There are many experiences that suggest their presence, but there is no hard and fast conclusive proof. Remember also, that "proof" and "evidence" are merely stages in an academic debate and are not totally incontrovertible proof positives. So, do we know what they can do or what they cannot? Do we have even the faintest inkling of their properties? No! But there are the strange experiences and they are valuable in their own right because they happen. Some people might say that the journey of discovery has its own rewards, and that is partially true, but others immerse themselves in belief and superstition on the way and then stop right there (in the beliefs and in the superstitions of the order of thinking that I have already referred to) and chose to not move away from that perspective. They stay separated from reality and chose to avoid challenging their own beliefs and experiences. They chose to stop growing, remaining in a spiritual Peter Pan life full of beliefs. Their minds happily satisfying their own beliefs about themselves, hallucination after hallucination mistaken for genuine religious or spiritual experiences. They search for "evidence" to back up their claims and the mass media is more than happy to see these people as a market to be sold to for profit. So, is the journey valuable? Maybe if those on the journey carried on travelling it and were humble enough to believe that they could be wrong and to stop broadcasting their half truths to the world, then maybe the journey would be worthwhile. However, as so many people seek comfort and reassurance that they are right, one would have to say that the journey is somehow incomplete.

Are the religions of this world true? Maybe or maybe not. But even if they are completely false and there is no evidence for the original wicca religion, or it was historically proven that Jesus, Moses or any other prophet never existed, then it would not invalidate the path of education of the religions themselves. Religions are good as they and healthy for the mind as well as to act to help people cope with life, they have their place, but they aren't scientific truths.
Religious people need to accept that.

We have to start looking at occultism in the manner of a scientist if we are to be taken seriously and therefore we need to choose a non-religious attitude to these things, ironically, despite the fact that we sometimes need to act like a religious person and seek religious experiences using religious methodologies to help temporarily change the minds state in order to experience the phenomena in question.

But why is it that you are interested in any form of occultism? Was it to learn how to have religious experiences for the purpose of being religious or to have your beliefs confirmed, if that is the case then I can't help you. You will get your own reward in the faith that you have chosen and being an evangelist for any faith won't necessarily help you (socially, intellectually, morally, financially or spiritually!). And if you think that just because you have experienced something, that it proves the objective existence of that thing, you are sadly mistaken!

I am concerned with trying to be scientific about apparently supernatural phenomena, the things that are called psi or psychic experiences. As scientific as possible which means doubting other peoples claims to the truth. Matters of religion are not a part of this essay at all, apart from when they can be used as a tool to control or influence the mind for the purposes of having such strange experiences. Once you have finished this book you should have the basic facts about how to attempt to bring about one of these types of strange experiences.

The Secrets of the Sages are an irrelevance to this essay and the sceptical approach that I am giving here, so to is the subject of "High Magick". The spiritual truths of any faith are an irrelevance when it comes to exploring Astral Projection (seeing the phenomena as natural and approaching it scientifically) and therefore also Magick (as in the magick of tradition, the unempirical experiential art form that results, so it seems, in apparently supernatural experiences) as a proverbial Science, but actual "Art" of Creating Strange Experiences, and attempting to do so (and often failing to do so) in Conformity with the will.

So, what does exist? Well, you do. And you have a mind, a conscious mind. If you are unconscious then you would not be able to read this essay. So your consciousness exists. How does it work? Well, Science tells us that we have brain cells and they do stuff. Great! Now, how ELSE does the brain work? You might say "well, it doesn't work in any other way" in which case you will have fallen prey to telling a hard truth claim which is conditionally based on current natural science theories. The strange experiences of which I speak (including astral projection) suggest that there is *more to it*. What that is we can't say, but there is more to it. So how ELSE does the brain work? We don't know, but you have consciousness. Indeed it is a fact that your consciousness is affected by diet, nutrition and a wide variety of other factors, but you have it. It EXISTS (or seems to). Having a consciousness is like being in the possession of the whole ocean and not knowing all the life forms that are in it, owning the planet, but not understanding its ecosystems and weather. Having a special box of infinite tricks that has amazing properties, but not looking inside to at least get an inkling that there is more to you, more to the oceans, more to the planet than meets the eye.

As you start to progress in experiential experimental occultism, you will, however, have one thing proven to you, that there are more questions to ask. Not more answers, for how are you a mere singular human individual to know the entire workings of all the oceans, or to have total knowledge of the ecosystems of the world or to know all of tricks in an infinite box of tricks? More questions to be asked, not more answers given.

It is an amazing and awe inspiring journey when done systematically.

So, let us use an example, from above by illustration. You are handed a planet and you have limited time to understand it, say, three score years. Could you study the whole thing? No, but you could chose, let's say, one particular ecosystem, one particular mountain, one particular river and just study that. Do what you can with it and see how far you can go with it. So, with the Occult, lets chose one aspect, but one aspect that can be applied to all the other aspects of the occult to a degree. Let us select Spiritualism, and for the purposes of this essay, let us focus our attention on the strange experience that is Astral Projection. But first, let us continue on the path of getting clarity about what we are discussing first, before we focus one hundred percent on the subject.

4

People are terrified of the occult. Strange but true, people are terrified. Why? Whenever there is something that people don't understand or don't have enough knowledge about, someone makes something up and then spreads it as a rumour and that rumour then gets repeated by people who are frightened and it makes a big scary mountain out of a molehill. This is one of the many ways that conspiracy theories get created and operate as a social phenomenon. But if occultism is so non-threatening, then why are people afraid of it? There are some religious groups in the world today who are afraid of losing members, they create TV shows that are designed to portray the occult in a bad light, to make it seem that all forms of spiritualism is of the Devil (which is laughable considering that most occultism practised today comes from Christian roots and not pagan roots). Also, misrepresentations of religious texts become shouted from the pulpit, carefully written to make the congregation superstitiously afraid of the possibility that the priest could be wrong. Powerful mind control techniques using fear to control the population! Also, occultists are not an innocent party in the mind control warfare. Some of them feed off the fear, they stop pursuing spiritual matters and instead just want to follow money and try and find ways if creating an absolute out of something which by its very nature is ambiguous. From the illusion of an absolute black and white truth they find ways of making profit. The exercise works very well for them, and from the muddling of people's minds they confuse the debate about what is real and what isn't and try and big themselves up to the point whereby they can comfortably retire having done more harm than good in their time in the public eye. Although I am all for capitalism and I am all for people making an honest buck, I strongly disagree with the way that the new age world, the orthodox religious world and the world of the "sceptical" commentator has gone.

The New Age World has profited from the phrase "it works" when applied to any form of alleged spiritual activity, as well as a gross misrepresentation of the concept of science. The orthodox religious world has profited through spreading rumours and lies and the sceptical community has allowed their disbelief to get in the way of any rational research into the phenomena that has been placed before them. So far, no-one has been innocent.

The danger comes not from the action of attempting anything supernaturalist at all, but from the thoughts that the activity creates in the mind of the person, and by activity, I also mean research or reading the writings of other occultists, many of whom were wrong in their approach and method. The danger comes not from researching into the paranormal, but from the interpretation that one comes to when one reads the writings of any paranormal writer. The danger comes not from reading the beliefs of a great but long dead occultist, but from believing what that person said in their writings. The danger comes not from reading the debunking of another spiritualists work by a sceptic, but through believing that because a sceptic has debunked the views of a person who had very poorly thought out beliefs and didn't understand what the hell they were talking about, that everything to do with the alleged phenomena is untrue. The danger comes not from experiencing any phenomena, but from the interpretation that one cones to as a result of that phenomena.

For instance, if I was to set down to do a seance using a Ouija Board, but I have heard many superstitious stories and have listened to people who believed that the Ouija device was a gateway to hell or some such nonsense, I am sure I would have a ghastly time with it and would associate any misfortune that I get in life to that one time, despite the fact that the seance has nothing to do with anything. Or if I read Crowley's Magick in Theory and Practice and as a result of reading his definition of magick, I decide (quite incorrectly and contrary to what Crowley was actually saying) that whatever rituals I did would be one hundred percent reliable and that I was being a scientist when I wore a rope and waved my wand around in a circle of candles, I will either drive myself mad or be very disappointed. Or maybe one reads the selfsame book and becomes convinced that, Yes! One really can not only experience entities, but reliably make them do what you want! You will either go insane trying to prove that same point to yourself (despite the fact that you may be older in years and better educated than Crowley was when he wrote that book) or you will end up believing in that "fact" as if it were a religious doctrine. Or maybe you watch a TV show in which a commercial psychic's truth claims are put to the test and then it turns out that the psychic was a fraud, you decide then that all psychic phenomena (despite the vast and growing body of knowledge on the subject) is rubbish. You would again be deluding yourself as you had been spoon fed an absolute and you have fallen prey to believing it. Or maybe you do an occult ritual after many months of preparation and an Angel appears in grizzly and demonic form and you get convinced on the strength of that very real experience, that angels and demons are real objective entities and have to be obeyed and worshipped, despite the fact that a strange experience can only prove the strange experience can happen, but CANNOT and DOES NOT prove conclusively that which the experience suggests.

All of these are examples of a delusional mind, all of them are proof that no matter how good your intentions, you can fall prey to weak minded thinking and you have the capacity to lose your reasoning ability. All of these examples show us quite clearly that all of the absolutes are falsehoods and that we cannot use them if we are to class ourselves as intelligent human beings who have a real and genuine interest in exploring strange experiences.

I can draw the horse to water, but I can't make it drink, but, for those who are willing to work hard enough to get the strange experiences, in accordance with my own personal experiences, the experiential proof that one can actually have these strange experiences is definitely out there. But the promise of strange experiences that I am offering is a different claim to that of other occultists whose obsession is more to do with proving the objective existence of the entities that belong to their own religious point of view. I feel that this is wrong.

My claim is that strange experiences seem to happen.

That is all.

I cannot claim that spirits exist, although I have had experiences that some people would use as evidence of the existence of spirits. I cannot claim that there is life after death although I have had experiences that seem to suggest the possibility. I cannot claim that telepathy is real despite the fact that I have had experiences which seem to prove it unquestionably. And many more experiences I could name.

These are experiences. All that I can, if I am honest, say, is that I have had a strange experience of a type, quality and order that our culture labels in a certain way in accordance with some spiritual beliefs or mythology of our time.

It would be dangerous for me to think any different. It would be likewise dangerous to question these experiences which have happened, as if I question the fact that I have seen something, then I might as well question the veracity of the existence of the keyboard in front of me. Like when I am in a dream I act as though the dream were real, when I do astrally project, then I act as though the experience is real too. However I can challenge what the experience (astral projection, angelic communication etc.) means. I don't deny the experience of the keyboard, and I act as if it were real. I see the keyboard every day therefore I treat it as if it were real. I don't see spirits every day, but when I have seen them I can say that the experience of seeing the spirit was real but I can question the existence of the spirit in question.

Strange experiences happen. They can be initiated though enough dedication to techniques from religion and magick, but the strange experience (such as an astral projection or the seeing of a spirit) doesn't necessarily mean that which the experience suggests. But, the very fact that I have had the experience can only prove to me that the experience can happen.

I don't deny my senses, but I can question the meaning of the experience. I can look at everything that ran up to me having that experience (which was **natural** as it happened in nature and **anything that happens in nature has to, by definition, be natural**) and attempt to, after many more attempts at having that experience, work out some of the factors that went into the experience and I can try and bring the experience about again. However, I have to be intellectually honest enough and humble enough to be able to say that my assessment of what seemed to create that strange experience might have been wrong in some aspect. Not necessarily entirely, but in some aspect. Therefore, I try my hardest to apply some scientific reasoning to my own interpretation of what happened. I am not a scientist, but I can try my hardest to think like one (after having spent years trying to learn how to think like a scientist as a result of research and hard study). Then, with repetition, self-analysis, questioning the accuracy of my sensory and cognitive perception skills, and more, to come slowly closer to the truth, knowing that as one man I can never be in total possession of the truth and that **it is morally reprehensible to make hard truth claims on a subject that has too many questions and no hard and fast answers.**

That is the way that I not only learn, but also keep myself safe and sane. The danger lies in many very human traits of thinking, and these traits have to be fought like a gladiator.

What about other dangers that people speak about? Does playing about with the occult anger God? Well, we don't know enough about God anyway to be able to say what his properties are anyway. I can chose to believe in a concept that I call God if I wish, but I have to say that that is only a belief, I don't know. I can cite many holy books as evidence, but that is just be citing the views of people who probably don't know what they are talking about, so I could be being false in my reasoning. I could have a transcendental experience that seems to prove that God exists, but that, if I take that as evidence for the existence of God is telling myself a lie as a strange experience by its nature ONLY proves that a strange experience can occur and doesn't necessarily prove that which the experience seems to suggest. It doesn't matter how many "real" God experiences I have, none of them are hard and fast evidence of his existence. So, if God doesn't agree with what I am doing then if there is any danger, that is potential rather then actual. And on top of that if God is forgiving and all loving, then, religiously (not in terms of social or legal conduct), it matters not what I do so long as I am a well integrated member of society.

Just for the record I do have a personal Higher Power or God concept that is based on Judeo Christian lines and with a Deistic component. And he doesn't care whether I am an experimental spiritualist or not. It is part of a system of contemplation that I use to help me improve my character, and through challenging literalism I can come closer to working out right from wrong. No, the bible is NOT the word of God, but the fruits of my contemplation, which is the strengthening of my conscience, by analogy and allegory, IS the world of God, but not in any literalistic way.

What other dangers do people talk about? Well there is bad luck. If there is to be bad luck or bad karma, one cannot say what the mechanism is whereby that bad luck or bad karma can be delivered to me, so it either doesn't exist or it is just a belief so it can be discarded. It is potential not actual.

What about a curse from some demonic force? If one can't prove the existence of God conclusively (which one cannot) then how are we supposed to prove the existence of demons? On top of that how are we to say that these demons can exert a force if we don't know their properties either?

Some people say that they have had a strange experience that proves Demons. Maybe they say "I saw it!". The argument of "but I saw it! Therefore it is real!" comes from science fiction and not from fact (some people watch too many movies and envy the fictitious characters in them) and if you think that science fiction or some Live Role Play inspired movie is some proof of occult wisdom passed on into the popular consciousness thanks to morphic resonance or due to some kind of spiritual intervention, you can't have attended any middle school science classes at all and plainly haven't got the smallest ability to use the brain that Nature in her infinite wisdom has given you!

5

What about the argument, that here are some things that humans aren't meant to know. Who on earth has the right to tell us what we can and cannot know? Once upon a time it was frowned upon to cross the oceans due to fear of sea monsters. Dragons were drawn on maps to scare people away from exploring further afield. Are you trying to tell me that we "weren't meant" to explore or to sail? If that were the case, why do you buy goods each week at the supermarket that have been transported vast distances for your convenience? Humans needed to break through the ignorance and stupidity of the superstitions of the people who perpetually told us that we weren't meant to know something so that we could have the advantages that we in the modern world currently enjoy every day. How much more can we learn if we are to try and study these strange experiences and to work out eventually **how we can use them** and what they say about us? They are part of our natural world just like penicillin and water.

What about the pagan argument that certain activities go against the natural rhythms of nature or what the God and the Goddess wants for us? The same argument that can be applied against biblical literalism can be applied to pagan literalism. We can't prove the existence of their gods just as we cant prove the existence of yours either (nor mine!), and we certainly can evaluate the properties of any allegedly divine being. On top of that religion has to be separated from science if there is to be any scientific progression. If that isn't done, no matter how many cell phones and operating systems we have got, as a global people we are just as stupid as the mediaeval peasantry.

What about the argument that its dangerous for your health? Although in some cases the placebo effect can exert a positive effect on the human organism, there may be an argument that there is some kind of negative effect too, namely that a form of danger can occur to the physical organism through psychological means, but if you have never been cured of the flu by a piece of lucky heather, you are unlikely to be killed by a man who claims that he can kill you with a thought. I have come across many people in my pagan days who claimed that they could kill me with a thought. Its quite amusing. If they could then they would have the perfect murder weapon and they would never be caught by mortal police men or detectives. However, either they never used it or they were just bad at it, or maybe it doesn't work the way that they think that it does. I am still here, alive and well which speaks volumes.

What about the argument that "it" is bad for the soul?

Well, you may believe in the soul, but that doesn't make it true and seeing as again we don't know the properties of the soul we can't say how something is going to affect it. So any "dangers" are potential and not actual. If the belief is based on religious texts then could the texts be wrong? Just as there are people who believe in them then it is possible that those who don't believe in them could be correct. We don't know and cannot know. We have no mechanism by which to know these things.

The more that you look into any argument against experimental experiential occultism, the more you realise that all arguments against occultism are in fact based on superstitious fear and paranoia, or if not that then plain stupidity and narrow minded thinking. And that goes for the arguments from atheistic groups as well as those from religious groups too, including and especially, those religious groups who use occultism as the "miracles" in their religion that they use to help generate faith.

But what about the atheistic arguments? Such as "there is no such thing as the astral body" (a point of view that is faith based, and on top of that it is hard to prove a negative so they are believing in a hard truth claim that is just as laughable as the views of the people who believed that they could kill me with a thought). So what? Strangely enough I am probably closer to the atheistic mindset as I know that even if I was to have a fully conscious astral projection every night, it would only prove the existence of the experience and wouldn't prove the existence of the astral body. A strange experience proves the strange experience can happen, but never proves the objective existence of the thing under investigation. But if astral projection experiences happen (which by my own personal experience **they do**) then they have to be natural whether they are useful at this time in our history or not. Why would it be that the allegedly "rational" atheists would want to stop research into something that is natural? Just because it can't be put into a test tube or accelerated at great cash expense to the European governments in a Large Hadron Collider, does that mean that research shouldn't happen into this field of natural science? There was once a time when a new form of radiation was discovered, a band on the electromagnetic spectrum. It was labeled as "useless" for a time until people started to find a use for it. That band was the radio wave band on which much of the twentieth century's science, engineering and technology was based and laid the way for television, the internet and numerous mobile and wireless media and telecommunication devices that we have today. That which is useless one day, we as a species will find a use for another day, but only once we have stopped seeing it as useless, in other words, once we have changed our attitudes to it and started to explore its potential.

On top of that, it requires little funding for people to have these experiences, much to research it scientifically, but little to experience it. Very little indeed. It is within the reach of most people (including the unemployed) if they have the capacity to stop being religious about the whole thing and to start thinking for a change.

Having said all of that, we still have to be incredibly thankful for the history of occultism from the ancient shamans, to the genuine mediaeval witches (religious experimental occultists), the birth of the spiritualist movement that started at around the time of the American Civil war, the refinement of Christian occultism that happened in the 18th century and subsequent movements that have lead up to the creation of the New Age movement in the 20th century and on to the more modern fad of Ghost Hunting as these things have brought a certain level of awareness of psi phenomena, but we have to be intensely critical of these movements for misrepresenting the ideas that they have carried to the point whereby they have retarded any intelligent research into consciousness.

Was sylvan Muldoon correct when he said that he had proof that he was immortal as a result of his experiences with astral projection? Certainly not! Was Crowley morally or intellectually correct to speak of beings and entities as if he had the ability to reliably extract facts from them or that they actually had a similar quality of ability to influence the world as you or I? Definitely not! These ways of expressing thought through language are proof positive of an intellectually flaccid mind that cannot assess the experiences that they have had. These people may indeed have had the experiences, Muldoon with astral projection, Crowley with spirits, but there is no way of proving that those things that the experienced actually meant what they seemed to suggest.

But, strangely enough, those same experiences can and do happen. My life experiences are testimony to this.

We mortals will NEVER **fully** understand this part of nature, we are like ancient sailors on the shore of a massive ocean. It is when we lose fear of the sea monsters that we can bravely explore the sea. It is only when we ignore the stories of what might exist or what might not exist out there that we can finally work out what does exist. It is only when we ignore the mythological stories about where it all came from, that we can genuinely work out the origin of the species of the astral realm's inhabitants (if any). It is only when we stop listening to the allegedly intelligent people who say that there is nothing beyond the horizon, that we can genuinely attempt to explore beyond that horizon.

A common question when it comes to any type of

strange phenomena is simply "how does it work?". It is natural for the human being to want to have some kind of answer especially if the thing in question is outside of the understanding of the human being in question. Either people want hard and fast facts if there are any at all, or they want a way of looking at the phenomena that seems to make sense to them and therefore they are looking for a belief, a kind of acceptable wisdom that seem to fill the gaps of knowledge. But what if there are no satisfactory explanations? What then? What if the only models of the way that this phenomena can work is not good enough or, despite the fact that they might make some sense to those who have only a very basic level of knowledge about the more esoteric forms of science, might be logically flawed to those who have a higher degree of education associated with those sciences? Would me giving you a belief actually help us as a species to progress in our understanding? Probably not. The moment that a justification is given, that is when we are staring in to the abyss of the discrediting of the phenomena that has happened, and although we may not have intended to discredit our own argument, the moment that we give a representation of that expression of "how it works" we have cut off our nose despite our own faces. The justification is taken to be the facts, and the justification gets challenged and destroyed in the minds of some people and that is then regarded as proof that the phenomena is false or doesn't happen. We have to be more honest when it comes to this phenomena, and all other forms of "psi" phenomena if we are to be taken seriously at all. We have to say that we just don't know how it works. Although the more strange experiences that we have may start to point to any number of possible hypotheses such as string theory, the holographic model of the universe, omnipresent consciousness, bioplasma and the like, these are just models (beliefs or justifications and are therefore an irrelevance) and no matter what, there is always going to be a counter argument as to what has occurred. After a sufficient quantity of experiences, we become sure that something is happening, but much more than that we are at a loss to say. When we as a species start to explore a new world, we have to find out more about it. We have to immerse ourselves in that world. The biologists have to learn as much as they can about the body. Experiment after experiment has to be done to the exacting standards of the relevant science. But when it comes to astral projection and the allegedly supernatural, countless pop culture mediums, spiritualists and other whack jobs make their solid hard truth claims about how the entire supernatural realm operates. Each one of them doing quite nicely (financially) out of the industry, but in the meantime they are leading the general public astray.

Let me illustrate this point for a moment with a hypothetical situation. Let's say that there is a country that I have never heard of, one that is many many hundreds of miles away. I have never in my life been there and I have never read anything about it and haven't seen anyone from that country at all under any circumstances. I get hired by a magazine to be a journalist in that country for just two days. I take with me a sketchpad and a few writing implements and set about interviewing a few people in that country. On returning to England after having only spent a few days there I could have a few diagrams and a few stories to tell, but that's all. If I was to come across a multitude that has not heard of this country at all, I could impress them with stories of the flora and fauna, of the people, their ways and their customs and more. But if I was honest, I could only tell them that which I have seen and heard second hand by a small handful of its residents. It would be morally and intellectually wrong for me to talk as one who has dedicated many life times to the study of that country. Now lets take that hypothetical example and draw a parallel with the real world. We have people who have never dedicated their lives to the study of theoretical physics telling us that there are quantum physics reasons for the workings of the spiritual universe. That there is a holographic representation of ourselves in another dimension and all that jazz and then saying that the reason that this psychic stuff has any real effect is because of these newly discovered sciences. That is madness. There are too many things that we don't know so how can we justify out beliefs (if we have any at all) using sciences that we have only got a very basic, and probably rather flawed, knowledge of? We cannot. We can say what we have seen or experienced and we can try and share the experiences with others and tell other people what our opinion is of these things, but we can't go any further than that.

So does it work? The answer to that would be that the use of the word "work" is misplaced. There are some strange phenomena that seem to happen under some circumstances but we still don't understand every-thing so we can't say for sure. New agers love the word "work" or "works" as the are always telling eve-ryone that "it" works. This is faulty in its reasoning and actually a deceptive expression of what is real.

Think for a moment about how normal people use the phrase "it works". They apply it to a car that starts on the first turning of the ignition key, or an electric light that always shines the moment that the electric switch is thrown. Thus the phrase "it works" is laden with meaning as people only use it in a certain way. It would be misplaced to use the phrase "it works" (a phrase that sums up in the mind of the reader or lis-tener, an image of total and complete certain results happening with minimum effort) when applied to a second hand car that's eighteen years old and is rust-ed to hell and back that does work perfectly well, when it wants to, and only one in a hundred attempts at starting it. It would be wrong to use the phrase "it works" to describe an electrical light that does work perfectly, but only sometimes when the faulty wiring is somehow in the right condition, the relative humidity is just right, nobody walks over that squeaky floor board and there is an "R" in the month.

Normal people don't use the phrase "it works" to human skills. We don't say "if you stand on that running track and run you will get the gold medal for sprinting in the Olympics, it works"! We say, if you are a fit and healthy person with talent and a natural physiology for this sport, who does the right training over many years, looks after your diet, nutrition, exercise and sleep and does everything that you can in accordance with what all the wisdom that we have as a species about the subject of sports science, you have a chance of running fast enough to get on the Olympic team and if you look after yourself you could do quite well". So from this you can see that the phrase "it works" is actually the wrong one to use when we are talking about human skill. As such new agers are probably the worst people to talk to when discussing their own subject. Shame really isn't it?

So does standing on that running track "work"? No it does not. Running is a human skill and it is variable. So, does astral projection and other psychic phenomena "work? No it does not. Astral projection and other psychic things seem to be human skills, are variable in reliability and seem to have even more factors that can affect them than running can.

But just as it is possible occasionally for a member of Team Great Britain to win an Olympic medal, so to it is possible to have a strange experience of a seemingly paranormal nature. But, this is a game of probabilities, and if you train more you are more likely to have the strange experiences that are needed to make something strange happen, or so it seems.

Now for the part of the essay you have been waiting for, the actual subject of Astral projection. Starting from the folk traditions about the spirit body and then working on to training and methodology.

Every culture around the world, from the most ancient to the most modern, has some kind of mention of a particular concept, either the separation of the soul from the physical body or the existence of a second body of sorts. Because these concepts are so universal and between groups of people and tribes that have had little or no contact with each other during their formative years, makes us want to ask more questions. Is it true or not? Just because this concept is religious does it mean to say that it is true? Or is that proof that it is false? We cannot say. For some religious concepts can be proven to have a historical or scientific basis in fact (such as the flood in the Bible and history proving that there was a localised, but not worldwide flood in that region at that time), but not all of them. This concept, the concept that there is some kind of spiritual body that resides within the physical, is seemingly universal. From the Native American Indians to the Ancient Chinese, from the Inuit or Eskimo peoples at the pole to the tribes peoples of the Eurasian continent and Australia, this belief of the existence of the spiritual body can be found.

6

One of the places where we can look for some hypothetical evidence for the existence of experiences that are akin to or similar to an astral projection is the near death experience. NDEs (Near Death Experiences) are in fact quite common and hundreds are reported every day in the USA alone meaning that there may be tens of thousands each and every single year. There are even support groups that have been created to help people come to terms with them and how they have changed the lives of the people who have had them. For the would-be astral projector, the NDE provides some useful research for those who want to walk outside their bodies, but under no circumstances would I suggest that you try and damage your body for experimental purposes! These things can be there to help you research what you might experience and indeed to allow yourself to intellectually explore the experiences that are mentioned in the anecdotal reports when you are attempting them in some meditation exercises we will look at later in this essay.

NDEs are defined as a lucid experience (namely similar to that of waking consciousness) which occurs at a life threatening event. They are not uncommon at all. They often happen when the body is in an unconscious state, but when the brain *doesn't* have an abnormally low level of oxygen in it. NDErs report having a sense of being somewhere else, not being constrained by the body and somehow being outside of themselves. It is often a very vivid experience. Sometimes voices are heard and conversations had with people who seem to be outside of the body, deceased relatives or angelic beings or guides can quite often be experienced in an NDE. A tunnel of light is often seen, but it varies in terms of dimensions and appearance from experience to experience and often leads to a seemingly heavenly realm or to a place of light where the NDE experiencer may have to make a decision to return to the physical or to stay in the spirit world. It is a global experience and no respecter of belief in God or lack of it, and no respecter of what culture, faith or economic status you come from.

As the person enters the NDE, they might feel their body "shutting down" or their vital processes coming to a stop. There can be paralysis too. The sense of separation of consciousness can happen early in the NDE, and about one third of NDE experiencers, so it is said, can observe events such as the doctor pronouncing the death of the patient from outside the body. This can sometimes be connected to a sense of being in the upright standing position but somehow floating above the floor. Seemingly consistently the NDE experiencer reports being in the same state of wakefulness as they do when totally healthy, alive, conscious, awake and sober despite the fact that the experience is that of being outside of the body. When in the experience, there is no sense of danger and nothing to be afraid of. Sometimes the NDE experiencer sees everything through a grey white or a blue yellow cloud (which connects nicely to some of my own personal experiences with out of body experiences).

What I like about the NDE from a research point of view is that it shows us that there are some kinds of strange experiences that can happen that seem to give us some kind of evidence of the experience of existence outside of the physical body (experience being different to fact). But we must always remember that "Proof" and "Evidence" are just stages in an academic debate. In this particular debate, that of consciousness existing outside of the physical body, there are more questions to be asked and therefore the proof has merely shown us that there are some things that do just happen. It is rather amusing to note that there are some PhD qualified scientists who use their research into the NDE to back up their belief in a spiritual body as an objectively existing object. But, a belief is just a belief and as such one has to say that whether one thinks one has enough evidence to hold that belief or not, that thing that is believes in might either exist or not as the case may be. It's not one hundred percent conclusive even if you are a believer.

We can't use these reports to prove that there is a soul or a spirit world, but the experiences happen and they are curious.

Another thing that can lead us to be curious about the possibility of the astral body is the number of forms of folklore regarding spirit doubles. There is a class of folklore spirit called in German, the doppelgänger or "double walker", in the Scandinavian countries a similar mythological entity is called a Vardoger, the Finnish people call this creature an Etiainen. In each case the interpretation of the spiritual entity is somewhat negative. The being may either perform the actions of the person in advance prior to some misfortune, or it may be a harbinger of death, disease or something equally unpleasant, but it is not necessarily regarded as being the consciousness of the human individual outside of the physical form, but a separate being, an evil twin, so to speak. It was said that Abraham Lincoln had a doppelgänger experience that his wife interpreted as being a prophesy that he would not live through his second term in office. There are also numerous examples of the doppelgänger being a spirit of misfortune in the lives of notable people through history. Was the doppelgänger actually an astral body projected back through space and time as a warning? Its hard to say especially if we are to look at these reports sceptically, but again there are many reports of this type that one might be forced to concede that a doppelgänger experience is not all that unlikely.

However, I personally haven't had one of these as of yet and what it means is another issue.

Whether the doppelgänger character is really one that we need to concern ourselves with when we think about astral projections in this particular essay is a moot point. The way that the character from folklore is written it seems to suggest that it is more of a Banshee type of mythological character, one that has been sent to warn or alert one of some kind of impending doom (maybe like one of the experiences I mention at the end of this essay in the section dedicated to my own anecdotes?). But is the definition of a banshee (from folklore) a class of spirit or a function performed by a spirit being? Again more questions and fewer answers. On top of that, although the reports might be accurate, one cannot trust the intelligence of undereducated people to make a rational assessment of that they have seen or experienced. Something is observed, it creates a need for answers, beliefs are created and the beliefs are considered to be facts which they are not. So the beliefs of the peasantry of an ancient time could be seen as interesting or a curiosity, possibly pointing to some kind of truth or maybe the way that people used to see the world, or pointing to the intellectual extrapolations that they developed as a result of experiencing some strange phenomena, but not necessarily the refined perspective of a person who has a more powerful honed reasoning ability, honed by a good education and a strong sense of inquiry. However, I might add that the modern day western educational industry hasn't really done much to improve matters considering there are people with PhD qualifications to believe in intelligent design as if it were a scientific fact rather than a theological belief, and that there are atheists who believe that if you criticise the intellectual fallacies of a superstitious person that is sufficient to honestly make a hard truth claim that the phenomena of which they speak or believe in, can't have any reality at all rather than just being a misinterpretation of something that could be real. **To destroy an argument is not to destroy the natural phenomena in question! If you destroy an argument about what is real in the world, you have destroyed the argument, but you cannot destroy nature.** If the superstitious or religious person has misinterpreted the or a natural phenomenon, one cannot say what they were actually experiencing. If you were to turn around and say that you KNOW what they experienced, you are being more intellectually dishonest as you were not the person who experienced the phenomena and on top of that who is to be the judge to say that *you* have total knowledge about nature? You don't! And the science upon which the sceptics rest their scepticism is malleable and prone to change over the years so they are basing their assessment on what is known and accepted today which will be discredited tomorrow.

More proof that we need to move away from discussing what is likely to be true in the allegedly supernatural and on to just trying to have the experiences, to describe the experiences and to state what has happened and to leave it at that.

There are other sources of intrigue too, including the more controversial. "Malleus Malificarum" (the Witch Hammer), the intellectually flawed medieval book written by a fanatic who wanted to create a political movement to kill off a certain class of people, namely Witches, and was probably written to help him expand his estate, seems to have some curious ideas in it that are directly connected to the idea of astral projection and indeed a correlation with some of my own experiences. It states that witches would, when attempting to explore the physical world or spirit world outside of their bodies, would visualise a blue mist or smoke coming out of their nostrils (and astral cable?) which would then form itself into a shape at a short distance away from their body, a shape of either an animal or human, and then, in meditation, the visualised astral being would explore the world. Maybe there were some genuine discoveries amongst the false confessions that were actually made by the Inquisitors? I certainly am not condoning the book itself, I think it is one of the most blood stained books in history and as such I condemn it, its authors and the fanatical aspect of the movement associated with it, but I also have a curiosity about some of the mythology in it. I have at times, used it in my own practices and had some interesting sensations and experiences as a direct result of its application. Yes, I do confess to having attempted activities that it is claimed, were done by witches in the mediaeval era. This included the activity of shape shifting the visualised spirit into animals, animals both from mythology as well as from the natural world, and have attempted to explore the outer world that way. Just for the experience, that's all.

It is such a universally accepted religious belief that it could even be regarded as "normal" to believe in the spiritual body.

7

Does the spiritual body exist? Purely on the evidence of the popularity of the belief, I would have to say that we don't know, as **popularity of a belief is not a scientific proof of something being true**. However, from the point of view of the occult explorer, the seeker of strange experiences, Astral projection, the process whereby it is believed that the spiritual body can be separated from the physical, and remote viewing which is like it, are some of the most experience-able "new age" phenomena that we can lay our hands upon.

Think for a minute. Would having an astral projection, a totally conscious externalisation of your apparent "spirit" body to the point whereby you can actually go for a wander about in the physical world, be proof positive of life after death, the astral body, the spirit? No, it would be a strange experience that science has not fully understood. But, and from my perspective, the perspective of a man who has had numerous different types of experiences with astral projection, the experiences can happen. So, again, lets focus on the experience and move away from religious argumentation.

The experience itself seems to coincide with some

types of telepathic experiences and instances whereby dreams can be shared with others, people who did not know that you were going to try the experiment on them, and often people who didn't even know that you were even remotely interested in the subject of strange phenomena.

The strange experiences prove that strange experiences do happen, but regretfully it is logically false to assume that having the strange experience is the final deciding factor in the debate about spiritual beings, life after death and the like. However, the strange experience in question can be replicated. Not necessarily as reliably as one might like (which is a pain to be honest), but it can be done, and I believe that it can be done by anyone and everyone. However it does take work, and humans are lazy and that often puts people off, which is a shame as the experience when you do get it, is mind blowing and leads you to wonder about human consciousness and whether we are really are our bodies or whether we are more than that.

I apologise for my reiteration, but this is a point that I have to get clear in your mind's eye. Having a supernatural type experience doesn't necessarily prove the existence of the supernatural, but that experiences can and do happen. I am afraid that you are going to have to accept my word on that. I cannot conclusively prove it in any natural science manner. There are too many questions about this type of phenomena and science has not given us any real hard and fast answers, but if we are to be good inquiring citizens of planet Earth, I see it as our moral duty to try and have these experiences and then to tell the world about them.

It is more important that we focus our attention more on the phenomena rather than any religious or metaphysical discussions on this one particular subject, after all, the strange experiences say something about us as a species if we have the capacity to have these experiences, and anything that happens in the natural world has to, by definition, be natural rather than somehow defined in any other subcategory that can be stigmatized against as a result of the continuing taboo against "psi" phenomena. Thus we can say that Astral Projection, or in this particular case, the experience of an astral projection (which should be considered to be distinct from any belief or religious discussion pertaining to the possibility of, or existence of, a spiritual body, the separation of the spiritual body from the physical body, spirits, angels, demons and the like, existing) is therefore natural.

So, when we attempt an astral projection, or we give ourselves a lengthy but flexible training schedule over a period of months or years for the purposes of attempting to gain some basic astral projection experiences, **we are not doing this to prove any theological or religious belief**. We are not trying to prove the existence of spirits, we are not trying to prove life after death or to justify believing any religion at all. We are merely preparing to do something natural. Just as natural as walking into town to buy some soya milk and lentils or to take a thermometer to some boiling water to work out what it's temperature is. All we are doing is attempting something natural.

Before you even start on your journey of trying to have an astral projection, I want you to be completely honest with yourself as to what you are hoping to get from the experience. If you are hoping to get a glimpse of "the other side" then ask yourself why? Will that help you to pay your bills or to improve your reputation at work? Nope. Will it help your relationships? No, not in the least. Will it give you a relationship? Probably not, and it certainly isn't a good way to impress your preferred gender. So, what are you doing it for? If it is for any other reason that just curiosity about this strange experience, I would have to say that you are probably not a good candidate for occult training. Too many people get too eager to have these strange experiences to give them comfort of life after death, to please their conceptualisation of God or to attempt to communicate with a long dead loved one. Don't be too eager. Remember that "evidence" or "proof" are just stages in an academic debate and are not hard and fast concrete proof of anything. All we have to go by are the strange experiences that we have, the strange experiences that are related to us by other people and the beliefs and folk myths (or religions) that are present in our society. Nothing more.

In order to try and get these strange experiences it is quite common for the newcomer to the occult to get themselves too hard and fast involved with occultists, people who say that they know, but in reality, these people who say that they know just have beliefs and a complete lack of ability to deploy scientific thinking to any strange phenomena that they might experience. Many of them are would be cult leaders and use the alleged authority of their alleged religion or beliefs to control the seeker of the truth. Some will try and confuse you with some scientific sounding language, references to quantum physics or other esoteric sciences and will try and explain themselves in these terms and sell themselves as scientists to you, but in reality they will just be would-be cult leaders or bullies who get a sick kick out of trying to control the weak or vulnerable.

Keep away from them. They can drive you mad with what they say and what they will try and make you do.

Be wary also of those people who try and tell you that the answer to occult activity lies in drink and drugs (including overdoses of legal drugs). I have seen too many would be occultists become damaged by drink and drugs because they were told of the "way of the shaman". In ancient cultures it is believed that the medicine man or woman would be someone who would be appointed as a spiritual leader of a tribe through the taking of drugs it is true, but funnily enough, in those days there was less of a knowledge of the effects of drugs on the body and brain. These days we know of the damage that substances can do, and in our society today there is more of a need to have tip top performance so that one can survive in work and socially. So unhealthy living is out of the question full stop.

Also be careful of idolizing the cults of the occult revival from the seventeen hundreds through to the present day (or of any era to be honest). Many of the members of those groups did take drugs, but they were just druggies, wastrels and hippies who didn't care for anything else apart from wasting their lives away. Some of the members of the classic occult orders were good though, but the Golden Dawn, OTO and other orders may have been influential in the foundation of the modern pagan movement, but only because of a massive misrepresentation of the classic occultists writings. In many ways there is more in classic occultism to confuse you than to help you because they chose to sell religion first and a scientific understanding of occult phenomena secondly (It is possible, for instance, that Mr Crowley himself first set out to educate people in how to think about these matters, but afterwards gave up and just sold religion as he realised that the people he was dealing with were pretty useless at thinking and religion was an easier thing to sell them and make a living out of). Also, as their interpretation of what the phenomena meant in practice was religious by nature, they lacked the objectivity to explain what they had experienced in any meaningful way. Modern Witchcraft, for instance, promises Magickal Knowledge, but they say that Magick is the Science and Art of Change in Conformity with the Will, which is a blatant and complete misrepresentation of what Crowley was saying. Crowley said that the "magick of tradition" which is what is practised in witchcraft and ALL forms of occultism and spiritualism, is unempirical and therefore not by the standards of the natural science. However the modern day witches will tell you that they are scientists and artists little knowing that Crowley was using the word magick in two ways, one to speak of normal mundane material life being done in a manner that is both artistic and scientific and the other to be the spiritual and religious exercises that were UNEMPIRICAL. So the "art and science" magick was doing natural science experiments, the process of writing a book, getting fit to do all work and the like, the actions of an occultist was the "magick of tradition" being experiential and experimental.

Most new agers even after having read Crowleys work many times over and are capable of quoting it word for word are incapable of understanding this

Nick Dutch

simple fact.

That is interesting in its own right!

Astral projection, being the subject of this book, is un-empirical and thus fits under the heading of "the magick of tradition" being an unempirical investigation into a form of natural phenomena that is psi, psychic orientated or to do with the mind (the term "psychic" just means to do with the mind and nothing to do with spiritual forces. Something esle that new agers seem to forget!), but not one that can be pinned down to being a natural science. But, we can but try to deal with it scientifically.

Now I have taken you though the equivalent of basic health and safety or a cockpit check when dealing with the subject of the allegedly supernatural (which in reality is just the natural, but poorly understood and the cockpit check in question was about making sure that you can think rationally about the subject), now it's time to think about HOW to actually attempt to have the experiences. Or to be more precise, how to familiarise yourself with the subject, set about self-training in preparation (Or should I say "how to attempt to have a strange experience that seems to fulfil the folklore definitions of what a certain kind of personal experience seems to have") The different kinds of projection and so on. We need to have a look at other peoples beliefs on the subject, the mythology of astral projection and that which has been corroborated by reason and my own personal experiences.

What follows now is some basics of the astral body and astral projection, some of which is based upon personal experiences I have had and some on research. The principal source book that helped me in my early days to have my first Astral Projection was "The Projection of the Astral Body" by Muldoon and Carrington, and in continuing with the cultural tradition that they gave us, I often alternate the words that I use to describe the astral body with others that mean the same or similar things in order to stop the exercise of reading this essay from being too drab.

It is said that the astral body is that it is a complete replica of the physical body that resides in one's own physical body during ones waking hours, some people believe that it is affected in terms of form and structure by one's self-image. Others believe that it can be shaped by certain visualisation and concentration exercises, for instance into the form of an animal or creature of mythology (as I have mentioned in the witchcraft example earlier in this essay, and as I demonstrate by way of personal experience in the section where I document my personal experiences) , in certain meditative states. During lapses in concentration in waking hours, ideally when at rest, it is believed that it can move out of co-incidence with the physical to a small degree and when we sleep or we are otherwise unconscious, it escapes the bounds of the physical body. Some people report that it is kept in touch with the physical with a cable that seems to be a kind of elastic, but the resistance of this elastic cable is reverse to rubbery elastic in that it gives more "pull" and resistance when the astral body is close to the physical form. Outside of a specific range, which varies from astral projection to astral projection and may have some connection to the level of physical health or energy of the physical organism, the cable exerts less pull and thus allows the projected spirit the ability to move with greater freedom of will. This chord range seems to be a matter of feet or meters rather than much more than that. However, personal experience has shown me that this is not only "real" but that the distance whereby the chord seems to exert its power is variable and that is dependent on the health and vitality of the physical body. As we sleep, so it is believed, the astral body acts like a kind of storage facility or battery, extracting the consciousness of the universe and tanking ourselves up with consciousness fuel for the waking day. The further our astral goes (but not too far!), the better when it comes to collecting the nourishing energy of consciousness. Conscious astral projections are rare because (so it seems) as being awake uses up energy and we need to get that energy from the Universe when nocturnally projected. In some dreams, the activities that we do with our bodies in dream are acted out in the astral world much like a sleep walker, but sleep walking, floating or flying in the astral body. So, as the astral world and the physical world are su-perimposed, in some dreams we are really doing those things that we dream of, but in the projected astral body. When starting an astral projection, the physical body is usually comfortable and relaxed with all the tension gone from the skin and muscles. The astral, which controls motion, is then free to be able to rise in accordance with the will of the experimental projector. Then movement is conjured up in the pro-jectors mind without tensing any muscles (quite a hard thing to do! It's like going through the processes of moving, walking and talking whilst the body doesn't move. Quite unnatural to us humans). The path that the spirit body takes is usually (but not al-ways), to rise a matter of a few feet in height from the resting body and remaining horizontal. (Again, there is no fixed distance value and it seems to vary from two to six feet) The astral cable extending from the back of the head of the spirit body and connecting to the forehead of the physical body, leaving a sensation similar to that of a heart beat at the back of the head of the spirit body. The spirit body then moves parallel to the ground or sleeping body to a distance that is at the edge of chord activity range. The spirit body will then descend to floor level (no matter which floor you are on in your tower block!) and will right itself, but the astral won't be completely free from the power of the elastic cable until the spirit body has moved fur-ther away from the physical body. So, if you are conscious and in spirit, you need to be thinking of moving away from the physical and not to think about what your body looks like. To be curious about your physical body can bring about the undoing of the astral projection experience and you may get a sensation similar to that of a flying dream followed by some falling sensations as your spirit comes back into coincidence with the physical. Sometimes this feels as though you are being yanked by your head or ears back to the physical body. This may naturally explain that flying dreams and falling dreams are hypothetically the spirit body moving. When being in the spirit body, you may find that your spirit body feels the same as your physical. You may not be free from your bad back or sprained ankle when you are in the spirit body if you have those ailments. But that does depend on the quality and type of experience that you are having. The astral body seems to move in a number of different speeds, one being just like that of normal day to day movement being walking pace, another being instantaneous and a third being like flying but faster than any jet liner. There may be variation on these forms of movement but they do seem to be the most frequent. Sometimes a sensation that feels like and sounds like rushing wind can be heard and felt when one is flying in the astral body. The same kinds of sensations as in a flying or falling dream, but kind of more so. When you try and walk through a wall or a door for the first time (and after!), you may feel some kind of resistance as if there is a sensation and sound like that of steam under pressure, as if the astral body is made of a vapour and the walls or door is similar to that of a fine gauze that the vapour has to force its way through. It can take some effort of concentration and passive but accurate visualisation to get the body through sometimes, unless you attempt to instantaneously travel to the location on the other side of the wall or door. Don't ask me why this is, I simply don't know. There are too many questions and to be frank, too few answers. So don't ask and just have fun having the experience. The astral representation of the physical world doesn't seem to have any shadows, as if you are seeing by the light of your own body or, that everything has its own light, a kind of blueish yellow light, and slightly creamy in colour. However its not always like this and it does appear in technicolour from time to time, but that seems to be partially in dream state, sleep walking in the astral body, or only a semi-conscious projection (that we will cover later on in this essay) and not totally in clear wakefulness. Sometimes you can trust that which you see and sometimes you cannot. That depends on the depth that you seem to be projecting which is not always in your control. It seems that objects leave an imprint and you can see that imprint but not always the objects in location. For instance if you are asked to project to a friend's house after a refurbishment and they have always had a certain book case in a certain location in a room that you have never been in before, say for ten years, and they have sold and got rid of that book case the day before the projection, you may still see it in that same room and that same place even though it isn't there anymore. Maybe even with the same books on it and you may be able to read one or two words that are on the spines of the books even though both books and book case is gone. It is rare to see spirits in the astral world, but sometimes they do appear, and they can be summoned by calling them in the spirit world. I have never had any bad experiences from another spirit being and I can't imagine any situation where I could be damaged by one, and on top of that as we have nothing else to go by apart from the experience itself, we can't even say that they do exist despite the fact that we can see them rarely in the spirit world, so don't worry about them. Some of them, when you do see them, seem quite helpful and actually rather nice people. If you upset them or act inappropriately towards them you may get some nasty dreams though. God knows why, so you might as well treat them with the same respect that you do to normal people as you go about your daily business if you do come across them. There don't appear to be any "demons" or evil spirits at all in the astral world, so that's something else to not worry about at all. However, if you are the kind of person who gets worried about these things then maybe this exercise isn't for you. There is no point in trying to frighten yourself.

Now its worthwhile thinking about things that can

help and can hinder the development of the experience of an astral projection. In theory, if you do more to make the experience happen, you are more likely to be able to create the experience. But do remember that as with many things in the natural world, there is probably many more factors then I could list here that can affect the experience. Although there are certain groups who say that they can recreate the experience clearly and truly, many of them don't seem to know their arse from their elbow and couldn't reason their way out of a wet paper bag to be honest, so it is worthwhile being sceptical of other peoples or groups truth claims. I have based my understanding of the factors that seem to be "positive" to projection and "negative" against projection based upon experience and reasoning and not on the views of others.

8

Factors that promote relaxation, concentration and health of mind seem to be positive. I personally would suggest that you to pay attention to your diet. I am of the opinion that if your foods have been tampered with too much you may feel uncomfortable in the digestive tract and that can reduce the likelihood of comfort during projection attempts and thus to be projection negative. So keep off tinned foods, processed foods or those that have many additives. A diet that is low in protein (meats), easy to digest, high in vegetables (especially broccoli and other greens that are regarded as super foods) preferably steamed, and low in carbohydrates is ideal. In occult tradition, a vegetarian diet is preferred during ones training and attempts at generating these experiences and, that makes a lot of sense when taken from the point of view of internal digestive comfort and increasing body and brain nutritional levels. One might also add other aspects to one's life to improve the vitality of the body and general health to help in projection. Some regular exercise (including warm up stretches), taking nutritional supplements in whatever you feel you may be low in (see a doctor and a nutritionist about this and don't take my word for anything of a medical nature. I am not qualified to advise you!), and looking after your circadian rhythms in terms of getting to bed at the same time each night can also help. Having a meditation life can also help. Not only because it promotes relaxation, but it gives you the ability to practice the states of mind that you need when attempting to have an astral projection experience. Whether this is five minutes in your lunch break at work sitting quietly with a cup of tea in front of you or staring blankly at an opened book in a library, or more formally in a lotus position at home after work, some meditation practice can pay dividends in the long run as ones tries some exercises to attempt to make the astral projection happen, but be disciplined about it. What is more difficult and more desirable when one is in training is to practice ones meditation on one's bed lying on ones back or right hand side, but to do so maintaining consciousness and wakefulness as one makes the whole body get as totally relaxed as is humanly possible. I mention lying on ones right hand side as that is anatomically correct. If one is on ones left hand side, the contents of the stomach can push on the heart or the arteries that deliver oxygen to the heart causing an out of breath sensation or other discomforts, especially if one has an acid stomach or other digestive disorders. It is possible to project on ones left had side, on ones belly and in a wide variety of other positions, but that seems to be rare, or only when other factors override that particular negative, such as dizziness, fever and the like.

Factors that seem to be negative to projection include having too many stimulating foods or beverages. If you are a heavy coffee drinker, have much less in the afternoons otherwise it might affect your ability to get rested. Sexual desire is another issue as if the body is aroused and the heart rate increases, that keeps the astral in the physical. Not being tired enough, for instance if you have been sleeping in the afternoon and you still feel refreshed when it gets to bed time, that can create unsuccessful projections at night. Anger is an issue that we all have, but developing some coping mechanism to bring about serenity can be essential. Maybe there is more than one reason why we should never let the sun go down why we are still angry? Restlessness and worry can be problematic. If the thing that you are worrying about can make you want to go places in the astral then that could be beneficial, but to the most part it makes you mentally and physically uncomfortable so take steps to minimise your worries and anxieties. Finish your work properly, make structured lists of the things that you have to do tomorrow so that you can return to it in the morning and not worry about it at night. Don't be lazy, make sure that all tasks are finished well so you don't suffer from guilt and remorse. Live a good and moral life as best as you can so that you have a clear conscience. Get a good self-development program in your life so that you can be more on top of life's little emotional issues. Maybe, if you feel the need, become religious just to give you peace of mind. Financially live within your means so that you have no debt problems to worry you at night. Have enough work so that you always have some money coming in. Look after your health so that will be less of a worry as you get older. Basically lots of common sense stuff can be done to help reduce restlessness and worry. Also, as fear can get in the way a lot, be careful about the media that you consume. TV shows, radio, online videos, blogs and books. Anything that could make you afraid of the supernatural, dreams, astral projection or anything similar will affect you enough to make the desire to explore the phenomena difficult. Find ways of dealing with other fears that you might have.

To train yourself up though, having good visualisation skills seems to be essential, but these skills have to be understood and have to be practised in meditation. One can develop these skills, but one can also replace them with other skills so long as one has a good fantasy life that is geared to projection. Don't be in a dream world when working, socialising or driving!! There is a time and a place for everything and there are probably more important things to be doing in your life at any point in time such as working, looking after your family, going on a date or paying your bills. If you are the kind of person who likes cheesy bad quality science fiction movies, then watch them, but ones that are geared to the concept of spirits or out of body experiences and won't make you afraid of the subject if you can. If you are someone who doesn't believe in the possibility of the existence of a spirit world, the astral body, ghosts and the like or has a very well developed sense of scepticism about other people's truth claims (I count myself in that latter category) then you need to be able to learn how to develop (at the time when you are attempting an astral projection) a certain suspense of disbelief. Although having a fantasy life is not essential, it can help. Try and get the balance right. Make sure that at night you develop a sense of obsession with astral projection. Fantasize about what it will be like, go over the path of the phantom body as it leaves the physical in your mind's eye before going to bed, write short fantasy story about astral projection, dictate to a voice recorder anything that you can about the subject of what it will be like and what it will feel like. Use the recordings when you are in a position of lacking faith and listen to them in the dead of the night before going to sleep. But, keep your astral projection life separate from your normal one, otherwise everyone who can't understand that you are just trying to explore a natural phenomenon will assume that you are somewhat bonkers. If you are busting a gut to tell someone once you have had some basic experiences then I would recommend that you keep a diary and record all of your experiences when they happen in the diary. This can be any kind, digital, or pen and paper, video or audio. But use that as your own marker of progress and don't try and see it as being some kind of scientific report. Science hasn't grown up enough to realise that there is more to life then just the physical as of yet, so that will have to wait till later in the emerging history of our species.

What else can help you to relax? Study yourself and work out what things are the best ways of silencing the mind and bringing about rest. Do you like essential oils or incense? Does lavender fragrance help you to rest? Why not use a lavender herb pillow at night to help you to rest or use the essential oil in an oil evaporator before bed (taking all necessary fire precautions and not leaving a flame unattended or burning whilst you are at rest or trying your projections)? My evaporator came from the local Pound store and was very inexpensive so you can get most of the equipment even if you are on state benefits. When I lost my evaporator, I fabricated one from an old soft drinks can, shaped a place to put the candle with a cheap pound shop pen knife and used a puddle of water in the top (the bottom of the can but upside down to make the top) so that the oil would be heated on hot water and not burn off at higher temperatures. What about new age music meditation CDs? I confess that I can't always listen to them as they aren't always to my taste and some of them are so damned nauseating that they turn me right off, but some which are not too bad can be quite soothing and help to take your mind off the noise of day to day life. But, if you start to get irritated by whale songs, then feel free to find some other gentle stimuli. Maybe white noise is more your sort of thing? If you don't have migraine or epilepsy, maybe you could look into binaural beats and learn which frequencies are best for meditation induction. They are a great way of altering your consciousness without drugs and they can help in training you in meditation.

Rehearsal is also important. Work it out. How you are going to do the projection. Get familiar with the whole process. "Walk" yourself through it in visualisation or even physically around the flat, apartment or house where you live. Tell yourself "As I fall asleep, I am going to start from my bed, rise parallel to my sleeping physical shell and then slide though the air to Here and then slowly descend and right myself so that I am standing up Here. I hope to be outside of chord range here and thus standing may be a little easier. However, I will take mental notes of the sensations and if I feel. If I think that that the chord is pushing my head or body, I will, in further attempts, try and stand upright further away from the physical body. I will then walk down to here where I will attempt to resume waking consciousness in the astral body". The more that you practice it, despite the fact that the repetition of the mental rehearsal may get tedious and boring as you carry on practising and don't get the results that you want, even though it is frustrating in the extreme after many months or years (it took me two years to get my first full conscious astral projection experience, but when it came it was mind blowing!), you MUST do it, keep the rehearsal and exercise going every night. Be obsessed in the last few minutes as one goes off to sleep. Make it happen!

As you go through the process of struggling to have your first experience, you may come across many obstacles that are in reality, based on your views, fears and anxieties. One of the common ones is that of doubt. Firstly, doubting is healthy. It is superior in every possible way than blind belief or acceptance when it comes to maintaining your sanity, but you are trying (when you attempting to do an astral projection) to create an experience, that's all. You have no proof of the existence of the astral body, no scientist can or has proven the existence of such a thing, not completely conclusively anyway. You might even think that attempting to have an astral projection is silly, but thinking like that can be detrimental to your success. It's a question of a suspension of disbelief, a suspension of doubt or maybe a trust in visualisation for the sake of visualisation. If you don't believe in the astral body, but you do believe in creative visualisation, then do a creative visualisation or tell yourself that that is what you are doing when you are lying in bed at night or when you are in meditation. There is nothing to stop an atheist or sceptic from attempting this exercise, if the atheist likes meditation. After all, what is so different to visualisation exercises if you just accept a naturalistic interpretation of meditation? If you are dogged by the idea that what you are doing is "silly" then stop telling yourself that you are trying to send your spirit outside of your body, stop trying to tell yourself that you are attempting remote viewing and just spend time working on the exercises of visualisation of projection rather than visualisation to project, instead. If you are an atheist or a sceptic then use this just as a series of exercises of concentration and meditation. After all, if you NEVER get an astral projection (an unlikely eventuality in my opinion), what harm is there in doing some meditation or relaxation exercises? It will probably do you some good! On top of that, if you get insomnia, are you going to waste your resting time through being awake or are you going to attempt some meditations to help you at least get some rest? And if out of body experience meditations are ideal for starting dream experiences, then they are probably a great way to help either get back to sleep or to give you some rest to help be a substitute for deep natural sleep. You haven't got an excuse to not do astral projection exercises.

To help you to relax sufficiently to allow the apparent astral body to escape the physical, you need to learn how to make the entire body relax. You can use a kind of meditation exercise to make that work. The one I am about to describe is in fact a very useful one. One that I am of the opinion that everyone should know and can make it easier to get rest when needed. You can do this one seated or lying down, it can be the precursor to meditation or maybe attempted projections. Some people use this kind of exercise as part of their religious practices, but for others its just a part of healthy living. It helps to train you in body awareness, the creation of physical self-image creation which is important as one attempts astral projection, but is also important in other exercises which are like it. It can help to bring about the ability to do meditative concentration and visuo-spacial awareness visualisations. All pretty beneficial for the would be projection experience experiencer.

You are lying on your back and are comfortable. You breathe slowly in through your nose and out through your mouth in a natural rhythm. Be aware of the sensation of the cold air entering into your nose and the warm humid air exiting your mouth. If you prefer you can do all your breathing through your nose. It is important that you be comfortable. Just for a few moments keep the attention focused on your inhalation and exhalation and the sensations of the air entering the body and exiting the body. Allow yourself to "arrive" in the moment of just being there, holding the concentration (not straining) passively, calmly on the sensations of breath. Once you get used to the sensation of this kind of passive relaxed concentration, you can then apply it to other things as we shall see.

Now change the focus of your attention to your chest area, to your heart. You may not have been as aware of the heart beat until you concentrate on it. It is about two or three finger widths above the place where the ribs divide and slightly to the left. Be aware of it, use the same kind of passive concentration that you used with your breathing to "feel" without touching, the pulse of life in the heart itself. You will soon realise that if you concentrate on it more, it seems to beat louder, but the fact is that it isn't beating louder, it is just that you need to keep your attention on it to feel it. Stay there for a few minutes, feeling the presence of the heartbeat. Hold the attention there for the moment because you are now going to attempt to experience the heart beat in other parts of the body and to build up a deep subconscious model of your own body using the heart beat as the main method.

Start at the top of your head, the crown area. Feel it just as you felt your heart beat. Know where it is. Hold your attention on the crown area. Feel in your mind's eye, the scalp, the skin, all things connected to it, the top of the skull and attempt to feel the circulation up there. That's right, feel the heart beat in the top of your head. Hold the awareness there, the calm passive but aware focus, on the top of the head and feel the blood pumping through the veins and arteries in the top of the head. Once you are there and you have that sensation, hold it for a few minutes, hold the concentration at the scalp. Talk to it in your mind's eye, and tell it that you want it to relax, to release the stress, to let go of the stress and tension of the day. You may not feel it happen, but do it anyway. Some people may even want to visualise the stress as some blackish cloud that falls away and drains into nothingness. Now move on to another part of the head, the forehead and face. Do the same thing. Feel it in your own mind's eye. Be aware of it. Sense it in relation to the top of the head. Sense the pulse in it and tell it to let go of the stress of the day. Tell it, not out loud, in your own minds eye, to release the stress of the day. As the face is more prone to muscular movements, you will probably feel some release of tension, but don't stop there, feel the heart beat in the face and hold the attention there. Then move on to the ears. There are muscles around the ears. Tell them to let go of the tension of the day, let your awareness, passive, calm awareness, dwell on the ears and the muscles that connect to them. Hold your attention there and try and feel the pulsing blood around the ears and the connecting bodily tissue. Keep the attention there for a minute or two. Then move on to the back of the head. This is probably the most important part when it comes to projection. Feel the heartbeat at the back of the head. Sense the muscles and bones and let go of the tension. Hold your attention the back of the head and keep the awareness of the heartbeat there. The move to the neck and the jaw. Do the same. Use the heartbeat to feel the way around the body. Take as long over this as you wish, but the longer the better. Make sure that you haven't let a single part of the body go untouched by this exercise. Cover the chest, upper arms, elbows, lower arms and hands, do the abdomen, the pelvis, buttocks, thighs, knees and lower leg and finally the feet and toes.

Make a good study of how to relax. If you are totally relaxed, the experience can be rather like being in a floatation tank. You can lose consciousness of the physical body with greater ease, or if there are still some physical sensations (such as the bed under you) it won't be something that can trouble you and as such it becomes so much easier to make the experience of a projection happen or for you to be able to enjoy doing different meditation exercises for whatever purpose that you see fit. The heart beat relaxation exercise is very good and it seems to build up body image in one particular way, but this next one that I am going to introduce to you, because it uses the visualisation of light, and is another body shape awareness exercise, it can help to build up in your mind's eye something akin to what the astral body is supposed to look like, so it has its own special benefits.

Start off comfortably like before. I tend to do this one seated in an upright position on a chair with my back upright but comfortable, my shoulders relaxed but not rounded, and with my hands on my lap, pointing inwards slightly and relaxed. The angle between my thighs and lower legs are at ninety degrees (or pretty damned close to it) and my feet are flat on the floor. It is called by some people the Egyptian meditation position because it somehow represents the positions of the characters on the Egyptian tomb paintings (or was it that the Egyptian mystical revival of about 200 - 300 years ago still holds some power over the populace? I report, you decide!!).

Keep the eyes closed and breathe in and out through your nose. If you can, try breathing in through your nose and out through your mouth. Bring yourself to the point of being able to start the exercise slowly. Arrive in the moment. Allow it to happen.

Start by visualising a ball of light, it starts off as a point of light just above your head, maybe 30 centimetres above your head, it develops an aura that extends out of the point of light to about the width of your head itself. There it is, above your head. Hold the attention on it, the same kind of passive focused attention as before, but with visualisation. If you want, you can associate a sound to it, maybe a high pitched vibration, a crystal "Chiiiiiiiinnnggg" noise maybe. Something that is spiritual sounding and enjoyable. Hold the attention on the ball of light and its sound and move it down slowly. It enters the top of your head, the sensation as it makes contact with the top of your head is tingling, loving and somehow slightly euphoric. It lights up all the parts of the body that it touches. The ball of light descends into your head lighting up the whole head as it goes. The ball stays there for a second in the middle of your head before lowering itself into your throat. It lights up the face, chin and throat as it goes down. The whole neck is now illuminated as well as the head. Keep breathing as you do the exercise. Giving your body and brain oxygen can help during this exercise. The ball descends to the base of your neck and to between your shoulders. It hovers there for a moment. You are enjoying the sensation of your body becoming slowly illuminated and you are becoming aware of any tension or dark energy being pushed away or burned up by the ball of light. It starts to move to the left shoulder and fills the shoulder with light as it goes. It moves slowly down the left arm, through the muscles and through the bones. Pushing out the negativity as it goes. Slowly moving, purposefully moving down the arm to the elbow. Illuminating the arm as it goes. From the elbow it moves down the lower arm to the hand and then out to the fingers. Now your whole arm and hand are illuminated. You are aware that a second ball of light is spawned. It appears at the base of the neck and between the shoulders and it starts its journey to the right shoulder. It gives light as it goes, leaving a trail of light just like the last ball did, illuminating the body as it goes. It reaches the right shoulder and starts its journey down the right arm. Pushing negative energy aside as it goes. Burning up stress in its beautiful spiritual light. It reaches the elbow and starts to move down the lower arm towards the hand. It then enters the hand and illuminates the hand and fingers. Another ball of light gets spawned. It appears at the base of the neck and between the shoulders but this one travels down the body, filling the whole chest area with light. Illuminating the spine, the lungs, the heart and the whole chest. It carries on its way downwards into the abdomen bringing light to the entire belly and digestive system, pushing away dark energy and bringing new light into the body. It descends into the pelvis lighting up the whole pelvic region, back, front and inside. Now for the legs. Another ball of light is spawned and it appears in the pelvis and starts to move down the left thigh, again banishing darkness and stress as it goes. Visualise it bringing light, healing and love to the thigh. It moves to the knees and then down the lower leg to the foot. It fills the lower leg with light and the left foot with light too. A final ball of light appears in the pelvis and it starts it journey down the right leg, starting with the thigh and moving along, burning up stress and bringing light to the thigh. It travels to the knee, and then down the lower leg to the foot illuminating the foot and driving the stress of the day out of the foot.

Now your whole body is full of light and you should feel more comfortable and relaxed.

If you were to do these exercises prior to a astral projection attempt, you might want to, after you have gone through the process of relaxing every part of the body, to return to the back of the head and sense the heartbeat there. When you do your astral projection and if you are lucky enough to have a fully conscious astral externalisation, you might not have any other physical sensations than the thud thud thud of your own heartbeat at the back of your own head, so it gets you used to astral travel sensations. There might be an argument to say that it helps the spirit cable to allow you to have your projection experience. However, that is harder to say no matter how many of these experiences you have. But no matter what, with sufficient repetition, this exercise can train you to have a much better (for want of a better phrase) mind and body interconnectivity. Natural science tells us that if you train your mind in anything over the period of many weeks, the phenomena of neuroplasticity helps the brain to grow to allow for that activity to be done with greater ease. You train your brain to make it easier, so repetition on a daily basis and practice again and again even though it is mind numbingly boring, is probably a good thing to do. You need to be dedicated if you want to have these kinds of experiences.

9

Once you have managed to train yourself in relaxing, you then need to train yourself in getting the spirit out of the physical. You need to rise, to be able to know what the mood of "rising" is and to be able to create it. Every movement has a mood and you need to be able to conjure those moods up in your mind when the body is totally relaxed or on the verge of sleep. The sensation is similar to that of vertigo, fear of heights. It is accompanied by a sense of disorientation, as one has to be able to experience oneself in a place where common sense tells us we are not, namely outside of our physical body, and to have the suspension of disbelief that we are actually outside of our physical body. We can train ourselves in this in many different ways, the simplest of which is that of just trying to invoke the emotion of rising when we are lying in our beds or to tell ourselves a story of what it feels like to be rising whilst we are tucked up in bed nice and cosy, our eyes shut tight. Try it, maybe increase the sensation of disorientation through visualising one's self spinning slowly. Like being on a children's playground roundabout in an elevator slowly going up through the floors but also spinning slowly as one goes up. Visualise this slowly, feel the sensation or mood of rising, feel the sensation or mood of spinning at the same time, enjoy it to the maximum in a kind of masochistic manner, but still tranquil and slightly euphoric. The elevator goes up very slowly, slower than a normal elevator, but by bit it goes up and the roundabout goes round and round, just enough to make you feel ever so slightly dizzy. You know how high your spirit body has to go before it moves out sideways, and try and reach that altitude. You may get different sensations on the way, a sensation of being pushed or pulled or both. Ignore these sensations or enjoy them and carry on holding your attention on the sensations in a similar manner as you did when you were experiencing the heart beats in different parts of your body. The same kind of focused attention (maybe you can see why that exercise was so important!). You may also want to, if you can do this as well, have your attention on the back of your head and trying to experience the beating of your heart at the back of your head. That might come naturally and if it does then that can be seen as a good sign. It doesn't always happen, but if it does, just realise that that is a friendly sensation. Kind of like a proof that you are delivering the breath of life to the physical body. You don't have to use the idea of spinning, but it seems to be beneficial. Something else to persuade the spirit to leave the flesh. It can help you to add another projection positive sensation that can help. If you can't visualise yourself spinning, then try and visualise the room spinning or the bed under you spinning or another object like a large abstract painting above or beneath your body, spinning. It can all help.

The sensation can be frightening, but learn to enjoy it. It can at times be accompanied, if you are successful, by other sensations, such as vibrating, a banging of your head, a shaking or swaying of the body or something more intense than that. If you don't get these sensations then don't worry about it. You are training yourself. It can also be considered to be a good sign to have more in the way of falling, floating and flying dreams as you are going through the lengthy process of self-training in astral projection. You can at times get these sensation and even an astral projection like experience in your waking state whilst in meditation or while dreaming.

Training yourself in being disoriented and to feel that you are out of your body or something similar to that can be done with a mirror. Sit upright and stare at your reflection in a mirror that has been set perpendicular like a dresser mirror or a wall mirror. Try and out stare your own reflection while telling yourself that you are looking at the real you. You may get moments when you feel as though you are in two places at once, as if the spirit body wants to be behind the reflection. It won't necessarily give you a projection, but it can get you used to the idea of seeing your "real" self-outside of the physical and it is therefore a very real and beneficial training exercise. Try it each day for twenty minutes for a whole month and see what kind of experiences and sensations you get from it and try and incorporate those feelings that you get into your meditative and nocturnal attempts at projection.

Learning what it feels like to have that state of mind whereby you are trying to rise but without tensing any muscles, to work with that concept of what it means to rise and what it feels like to rise is important when it comes to moving in the astral once you are there. You will need to move your body of light by willpower, and that doesn't mean getting all tense, as tension and stress will act against the sensation of astral projection and will be projection negative. To "will" yourself to move forward is to have that mood or emotion of what it feels like to move forward as well as the desire. Once you have that mood or emotion, the astral will move forward. To "will" yourself to move sideways is to have that mood or emotion of what it feels like to move sideways. Once you have that mood or emotion, the astral will move sideways, and so on and so forth with all the other directions and speeds imaginable. You have to conjure up that mood in the mind and then once you have it you are doing it and without putting pressure or tension on the physical body itself.

I do hope you don't mind if I distract your concentration for the moment. I have been writing about the astral body and astral cable at various points in this essay as if these things are proven fact. Unfortunately, we can't actually say that we know that these things exist. This fact of what "we" do know and what "we" don't know has to, unfortunately, be repeated ad nauseam otherwise you may end up falling prey to being a "victim of illusion" as the occultists of old called it. Namely you will develop a religion based on the subject. We can say that my computer that I am using to type this essay exists to be sure, but the astral body? No. It doesn't matter how many personal experiences that we have that might convince us as experimental occultists, that might give us enough confidence to develop a strong belief that the astral body exists, but the fact of the matter is that the experience of an astral projection is something that raises questions and doesn't provide answers. The only answer that it can seem to provide is that certain types of personal experiences which fit some of the properties described by the definitions from popular mythology, seems to happen. And that's all. The experience seems to occur, which is strange enough, but what it means we will NEVER be able to say at all. It is so intellectually flawed to say that on the basis of the experience, we have hard and fast proof of the existence of the astral body or spirit beings that it can serve to discredit us. Instead of the global debate becoming about how to create this phenomena and how we as a species can use it in the future to assist in understanding human kind, our minds, our brains and bodies, or to assist with human health and communication, people go off on to the useless tangent of arguing about religion and different beliefs. Arguments that are by their very nature, arguments in a circle as no matter what, people from all sides of the debate won't be willing to concede that they might be wrong. All scientific reasoning goes out of the window and we end up with warring sectarian tribes attacking each other over cyberspace and no real scientific progression at all. Try and focus your attention on the experience and how to generate it. Try to use the descriptions that I have given you as well as the mythologies that I have discussed and the personal experiences that you are about to read as tools. Use them when you have taken yourself in to a hypnotic trance or as you fall asleep and use the ideas to the best of your ability. It is necessary at times to describe the mythological astral body as if it were real as you will be attempting to visualise it and use it in your meditations and thus you need to make sure that you have a good grasp as to what this thing looks like and what the properties that mythology says this body can do so that you can start to create some experiences and make them happen. Once you are "there" and have successfully got an astral projection, only then can you start to play with the phenomena, start to have new experiences, work out for yourself what it is like to really walk through a wall, to invade a sleeping persons dreams and how excited (or terrified) you will feel when the tell you what they have dreamed of the next day when you ask this person that you have not primed, what they dreamed of the previous night. It makes you wonder. Sure it can make you think that there is more to life then the physical, but to move any further than that is to move into the subject of religion and away from searching for the truth.

Strange experiences only prove that strange experiences can happen, they can't prove that which the strange experience seems to suggest. We have to accept that fact of reasoning. But the very fact that the strange experience (in the case of this essay, an astral projection type experience) does happen or can be created with enough dedicated perseverance, says something about us as humans as we have the capacity to have these strange experiences, but what it is that it says about us as humans we just don't know and probably won't know until well after yours and my lifetime. There may be an evolutionary component to these strange, but natural, experiences, there may be many reasons for them, but we will never know. It is therefore our moral duty as explorers into nature to have these experiences and to tell others about them just as I am telling you right now. I am of the opinion that we should be focusing our attention on the experience and how to generate the experience and to throw religious argumentation associated with these phenomena into the dustbin of history. And, yes, that means bringing the kind of thinking that was present in the Enlightenment period of European history into the unenlightened, highly sectarian, dogmat-

ic, fundamentalist and superstitious new age movement for the purposes of steering the members of that
community away from their appallingly unscientific
use of language and woolly thinking and to attempt
to bring some scientific reasoning into the unempirical so people in these movements can start to understand what the hell they are both doing and talking
about.

This perspective, in which I aspire to have and active-
ly seek experiences which are considered to be transcendental in nature, but apply reason and a modi-
cum of doubt to the religious doctrines associated
with the things that I am attempting to explore, is
called TransDeism. "Trans" from the word "Transcendental" and "Deism", the Enlightenment based school
of thinking that was both reason based and God centred. It is completely separate in terms of intellectual
basis from dogmatic religious literalism.

10

But back to the subject of astral projection. There seem to be different qualities of projection from the totally conscious through to the semi-conscious. It may well be the case (hypothetically of course) that even when you are daydreaming and thinking of somewhere that you need to be, at times, that you are actually outside of the body in a small way. Obviously this is hard to verify, but reports that lovers give of being able to feel each other's presence when they are apparently thinking of each other seems to make some sense. In some meditations that are out of the body oriented, such as a pathworking exercise, I do sometimes get sensations that show me that there is a possibility that each one of them is in fact an OOBE of a semi-conscious nature, despite the fact that I have some very obvious physical sensations.

If you are serious about wanting to eventually have a full astral projection, you need to practice on a regular basis, but that can get boring, so another exercise needs to be used to help you to keep in with some of the main skills but not to allow you to get so bored with the idea of a full astral projection that you don't bother with the idea or that yourself training gets too damned dull. One common exercise that has been used by occultists for ages is the "pathworking" exercise. As with many things in the new age arena, the word "pathworking" is a rather silly word that stands for something more normal than you might think. It is an imagined or visualised journey that it done in meditation. The thing that separates it from standard boring daydreaming is that it is done as a form of self-training, and you do it with the same rigour and earnestness as an athlete practising their sport of choice. You work on the moves, so to speak, so that when you are in the condition of wanting to use them for real you can and with greater potential success then otherwise. You use the same type of concentration that you used in the heart beat meditation, but you elaborate upon it, make it better and make the experience stronger. You take into account that you are attempting to do this for the purposes of having a full blown astral projection, so you attempt to make the visualisation, for want of a better word, the sense of your body, as clear and real as you can. You work on holding the idea of conscious awareness in the imagined body as if it was your physical body and you practice, during your many months or years of training, to do many different types of moves in the astral body, different rates of speed, different types of activity. Practice walking, floating, hovering, appearing and disappearing in different locations, sensing your consciousness in different ways. But you do it for fun and pleasure and again, don't see it as being some kind of scientific study, but do try and learn from it.

Learn the things that you find easy, the things that you find difficult and just as with any form of school work, try and work on the things that you are weakest at. I have been doing similar forms of meditation for years and I am still learning a hell of a lot as I go.

As you practice this exercise and become more creative with how you design the pathworking exercise, you may have some symptoms of a semi-conscious astral projection experience at some stage during the entire meditation. As should be quite obvious and should not need much in the way of elaboration, it makes much more sense if you are working up to an astral projection, to base the basic moves of the body based upon the concept of the movement of the astral in a real, full blown projection.

The storyline can be based on anything. Literally anything. Scenes from Star Trek, Lord of the Rings, the Blade series of movies or any kind of popular fiction that you are obsessing about at the moment. If you are a person of faith and have immersed yourself in the mythology of your faith then you might want to have a theatrical representation of meeting an angel, pagan deity or spirit guide. People who are more nature religion based may want to have a walk in the woods or garden as a subject of meditation. A Christian might want to have a scene whereby they visit a church, for instance, or a ruined abbey. It doesn't matter much what the story is about, but what DOES matter is that your body moves and you are going for a journey. Traditional pathworkings often start with a visualisation of the room around you disintegrating into a bluish yellow creamy mist (similar to the colours of the astral world) which then clears away to reveal either a door to another world or the other world itself. However, traditional pathworkings aren't geared towards training to have an astral projection, so one needs to be more creative about how one creates it. So, instead of just visualising a mist, one visualises the path of the spirit body. One can include the mist visualisation as well at any stage in the game, but it's the path of the phantom that you need to work with mainly. It would be more beneficial so it seems to make the astral body movements correlate with where you want the body to move to when you are doing a real projection and thus to treat it as part of the process of rehearsal. Only once the imagined body has appeared at the position of the end of chord activity range could you then visualise the mist appearing and taking you to the fantasy world in which you are practising the movement of the spirit body.

Remember that the operative word here is practice. If there is another one (for pathworking anyway) it is entertainment. You have to practice to get the skills up. Although being obsessed about doing it is a good thing as far as eventual success is concerned. Don't allow your obsession with attempting to get an astral projection get in the way of your everyday normal life, otherwise things get difficult. There IS a time and a place for everything and after all, your practices at projecting are a hobby and not your job.

I do recommend that you use the ball of light relaxation meditation before you start practising with a pathworking, but the heartbeat relaxation exercise is also beneficial. So long as an awareness of bodily shape can be built up, relaxation and proper meditative concentration can be implemented and you can start to feel that the process has begun, you should be fine.

When practising a pathworking or similar exercise, one can often fall into the trap of feeling upset or somehow disappointed that one has not had a more dramatic experience. Don't worry about that. Strange experiences will come, but you do have to practice.

I like to base my pathworkings on my own environment, my bedroom, my city, street and house. After all, I imagine that I will be walking about in the local area in the astral, so why not get more familiar with the local area and use that as a basis of many imaginary journeys. I take into account the path of the astral when it leaves the physical first and foremost, and then work up from there.

One of the symptoms that makes me feel that there is an OOBE or astral projection component to it experience is that when I visualise the travelling spirit body returning to the physical, I sense the body actually warm up, as if a spiritual cloud of life energy has somehow returned to the physical. It is a strange sensation. I don't know if that could actually be measured by some kind of infra-red laser thermometer as I have not tried. However, seeing as spiritual healing activity makes the patient experience warmth from the healers hands despite the distance of the hands from the patient's body and no temperature rise is detected, it may well be something that is felt and not something that is actually physically detectable. Conversations with other spiritualists show me that similar experiences are had by other projection experimenters and as such we can probably deduce that it is a common experience.

But it is practice that make it (for want of a better word) work and to understand what I mean when I say visualisation. It is not purely a visual sense, it is to hold an idea in the mind's eye that covers as many sensory sensations as one can. The shape of the boy and the way that it feels, the position relative to other things, as if you are actually moving the sensation of being about rather then just moving about an imaginary representation of yourself. I can visually imagine many things but they can be fleeting visualisations, not REAL visualisations or visualisations that are made to seem more real through adding more depth to the experience. If I can draw an analogy to digital media, we get immersed through audio, thus radio was great, we got more immersed through black and white TV which gave us more of a feeling of being there than just radio, but after that we wanted to get more from the experience of media and more suspension of disbelief so we got colour TV and eventually stereo audio and then surround sound audio and now 3D. All of these things were to increase our ability to "really be there" and to succeed in terms of our ability to feel a presence in the virtual world beyond that which could be achieved otherwise. Think about how you are visualising, how you can increase the "visualisation" sensation and how to make it more immersive through adding different dimensions to the things that you visualise. If you are to visualise being in a room, what does that room smell like? Can you sum up the smell? If you were wearing socks and not shoes, how would the carpet feel under foot? How is the lighting arranged in that building and how does it feel? What quality of colour? What kind of mood do the inhabitants of that building tend to leave in the place? What vibe of place is it? How does it make you feel? Where in that building do you feel that you are allowed to go and where do you feel that you are not allowed to go and how does that make you feel? Can you sum that up in your visualisation of the place? How does it sound? Is there a 50Hz electric buzz in the background or is there another buzzing noise created by the erratic fluorescent lights? Is there normally the sound of a tea urn boiling away in the background and in some parts of the room does the smell change from that of cleaning solution to milky tea and solidified sugar? What about the flow of air around the room, do some areas seem to have more drafts then others and is the heating on too high usually? Can you feel the radiant heat from the industrial heating units suffocating you in some parts of the room and does the cold air descend too quickly and seem freezing near the large plate glass windows? Is it clean or can you smell stale dust from the lampshades and the work surfaces? Is there an aroma of yesterday's lunch in the area? Does the shape of the room feel comfortable? All these things and more, if you can do it, need to be incorporated into your visualisation.

What about you? Your clothing. In your astral projection do you want to be dressed comfortably in clothing that is appropriate to the situation or not? Do you want to appear naked? In your dressing gown and slippers like Arthur Dent in Hitch Hikers Guide to the Galaxy. You might want to if the fantasy word that you are using is based on that set of folk myths. How about a suit? Do you feel awkward dressed that way or do you feel comfortable. How does that fit in and does it help with the visualisation? If it does then you have discovered something about yourself and what can help you (personally) to astrally project. At least, at the moment! This will change with time as you are interested in other folk myths or maybe just feel more comfortable dressed differently.

There is more to visualisation than just imagining what something might look like. Try and do it in three dimensions as if you are really there.

It is another skill that takes time and practice, but it can also be brought about spontaneously if the circumstances are right. However, what those circumstances are will be different with every person and their own body and brain. For example, there was once a time that I had such an allergy to coffee solids that decaffeinated coffee would always have a more powerful effect on me then real "full fat" coffee, and so my body and mind reacted differently to the foodstuff of real coffee. There were certain abilities that I had at the time that seemed to be totally dependent on the decaffeinated coffee, and as my body started to react differently to the coffee I got very different effects from it. Some new skills started to be developed, but others stopped being as easy to replicate. The same was true for me for other food stuffs so changing my diet and working out what foods are doing to me has become a way of life. But it also means that have a personal understanding of food science that is different and distinct to that of another person. I can't tell you that a particular mix of decaffeinated coffee and a certain type of fast food followed with an E number chaser of a certain type of confectionery will be the magic "flying potion" that you need to have the prerequisite conditions for astral projection, but I can recommend that you do try and develop a stronger more powerful introspective body awareness so that you can take note of what your body wants at any given time and then to work within those needs. Then you will find it easier, as you study yourself at the moment and how you and your body is changing, to do any task. Developing a mind and body awareness when it comes to foods that you eat, the air that you breathe and the water that you drink is in fact quite a healthy practice anyway and something that can hold you in good stead as you get older, so you might as well start now and use the desire that you have to attempt an astral projection to start this healthy exercise.

Part of learning to be a projector (as well as anything else in the allegedly paranormal arena is concerned) is to know what your body feels like it capable of doing at any given moment. For instance if you feel that you are more likely to ave a more powerful visualisation on any given night, then that is the night when you practice a projection visualisation and attempt to go and visit someone in their dreams, ideally someone who you will be seeing the next day, someone whom you can then ask what they dreamed of and then to see if there is some kind of correlation....

You won't always be able to read your own body right, sometimes there can be a change of bodily state that occurs without you knowing it and you may get it all wrong. You need to see whether your health was ok on that night, whether you were fit enough, whether you had a fever or had eaten something that might have disagreed with you.

But you can't just rely upon body state analysis if you are to be a success, it becomes necessary to try and learn how to operate beyond that and if possible (and sometimes it can be done and other times it cannot be done) to override the restrictions of the body through the power of the mind alone or indeed through alternative exercises that can have some projection beneficial effects. I have had some projection experiences using meditation and mantra alone and that has proven to be very beneficial indeed. Sitting it the lotus position (or as close to it as I felt comfortable) and doing a chant in English that seemed to sum up what I wanted to feel.

Mantra meditation to attempt to create an astral projection experience doesn't have to happen in any particular meditation position, it can be done lying in bed, on ones back on one's side or seated in any meditation position. If you do the mantra to yourself and not out loud, you can do this in a car on a long journey (if you are the passenger!), on a long distance flight or seated in a library staring blankly at a book (which is great if you don't want to do your practice in meditation at home due to distractions).

11

But what mantra shall you use and is your mantra just the words that you repeat as you are trying to enter into a meditative trance? It is what you "visualise", by the definition that I have already given, as well as the words that you use. So the "mantra" is in fact how you want to feel and what you aspire to experience. You are trying to get out of your body, so that means rising, floating sensations, being lighter than air, something that means "rising". You can choose many words or you can choose one word. Maybe, a good choice for you would be HE – LE – UM. Three syllables for the lighter than air gas that we use to fill balloons on festive occasions. Something friendly that we associate with fun as well as something that sums up the feeling of rising upwards. The mantra also becomes us filling our minds with the idea hat the body that we feel our consciousness in, steadily and surely getting lighter and lighter, or maybe filled with something that has some of the properties of helium gas. We can even imagine ourselves as the helium balloon and the string that the balloon is tied on with is the astral cable that tethers us to the physical body, an anchor or holdfast. Take your time over the meditation, don't rush it and don't rush to have the experience, just practice it and see how it goes. You wont necessarily get there on the first try but the more that you try at it the better that you will get at it. After you have tried this as a meditation exercise during the day for 20 minutes each day or longer for maybe two weeks to three months, one night when you are exceptionally tired, try it as you drift off to sleep, maybe after having done a body awareness relaxation meditation beforehand.

Mantra meditation is something that is a complex subject, and needs a volume dedicated to it in its own right, but for the would be astral projection experiencer, it is essential as it is all about changing the state of mind, having some influence over one's own brain waves and taking control. It is a valuable training exercise and is cheaper than investing in a mind machine. Also it helps you to reach the state of mind whereby one is more likely to experience something strange. It is widely considered in occult circles that people who do more meditation are more likely to be "psychic" or to have some kind of sensitivity to the astral world, or maybe to the energy fields of those around them. Meditations are also done by people who want physical health due to the practice at lowering stress and positively affecting blood pressure as a result of the healthy exercise of being a meditation practitioner. All kinds of health claims are made by the evangelists for meditation, but one thing is for sure, it can help to bring about a sense of relaxation and can also be used to assist in mind body interconnectivity. To become more aware of one's own body and what is happening in it. This is something that I have already mentioned, but I am a firm believer that it is a healthy life skill to develop.

To put it as simply as is possible, a mantra, or a set of words, sounds or syllables that are used by the meditation practitioner and are repeated continually for an extended period of time. That is all. It can be done with the eyes open or closed, but in my humble opinion works better with the eyes closed. Different rates of breathing are used in different ways, but, again in my opinion, you need only breathe gently as nature wants you to, unless you need to increase the levels of oxygen in the body. Your attention needs to be on the mantra and nothing else. As you start your mantra meditation, it is well worth while realising that you won't be able to quiet the mind immediately and for the first few minute of the meditation, it will be difficult, but not impossible to keep one's mind on the mantra. Don't stress yourself out about this, but carry on using it over and over again. If the mantra is lengthy and you make a mistake, don't tell yourself off about this, but calmly start again. Treat it like a skill that has to be developed and see how well you do. You don't have to become an expert at it (and after many years I still have days when I do my meditation and muck it up so don't worry). Gently observe yourself as you do the meditation, work out how you are doing it and whether you are progressing nicely or not. See how your mind starts off random and chaotic full of the argument that you had with so and so, the issues with the weather, trivial news stories and concerns about paying the bills at the end of the month and what you are going to have for dinner or what should be on your shopping list. Put those worries aside for the twenty to forty minutes of your daily mediation practice. Just keep the mind on the mantra. The sound of the mantra, the way that it echoes around the body, the feel of the words. Keep practising, not under stress, but through passive attention. Holding the attention on the words or sounds. You don't have to chant out loud. You can whisper or just hold your attention on the words themselves without uttering a single sound. What is important is that you do it, and keep it up every day, if that is the type of brain changing exercise you prefer.

If you are going to use mantra meditation for astral projection (or for any other aspect of occult activity) you need to think about the words, the pitch of the words, the effect that these things have on you, the sound of the words or of individual letters or syllables. After all, you are proposing to enter into a trance like state of mind in which ideas can be powerful and can change the experience of the meditation. Often the meaning of the words is subjective. For instance, the word "Lamborghini" might be tremendously exciting to someone who is interested in exotic forms of automotive transportation, but not to me as I have no interest in the subject. Using the word "mon-key" to help you to somehow introspectively connect with the energies of a monkey might work nicely for you but "My Mothers Monkey Makes Many Mistakes" might be so frivolous that you might just find yourself giggling and not doing any real in depth meditation.

I had a frightening experience once using mantra meditation. I had head of the idea of the Kundalini energy and that it was good for assisting in developing psychic awareness. So I decided to use "KUN – DAH – LI – NI" as my mantra. I started off in a practical meditation position seated upright on the floor and then started to chant. I started my chanting quietly, wanting to watch myself as I slowed down the mind and brought about hemispheric synchronisation, the meditation state of mind. I progressed with my chanting eyes half closed and something got me, so to speak. I felt the need to enjoy it, to really enjoy the mantra and I felt myself being swept up in the sounds and it was exhilarating like a dance or the greatest pop music in the world as I chanted "KUN – DAH – LI – NI" over and over again louder and louder. It was somehow intoxicating, and then I kind of hit a point whereby I could handle it no more and I fell into a lucid dream, my body falling backwards. A totally lucid dream that was as clear and real as anything that I have ever had in my life, as clear and awake as I am now writing this. In this dream I was being held by the arms and legs by some strong people, they seemed to be dressed in some kind of priestly garments of red and black and had golden chains around their necks each with a medallion that looked like a snakes head. I was being suspended above a coffin that was full of the writhing slithering bodies of many snakes. All of different colours and types. I tried to get free and in the dream cried out for help. As I did so I was dropped into the coffin and I felt the warm scaly bodies of the snakes beneath me suddenly become alerted to my presence. Some coiled around me and some bit me. I again screamed for help as the lid of the coffin became nailed in place and I awoke on my back in a sweat.

It is plan to me now that the kundalini manta was not for me at that time due to its association with snakes which at that time in my life I had a fear of. If you are aware of your own emotional limitations and how you personally connect ideas, then you are more likely to be able to select a mantra that is appropriate for what you need to achieve.

There is one sound that is ideal for many types of spiritual forms of meditation and that is the "Ah" syllable and derivations of it. It is used in church choirs to refer to ascending to heaven, it is used in movies to refer to anything of a divine nature. It sums up a feeling of something above one and something that is good and beneficial. Angelic, astral, somehow appropriately divine. One doesn't need to be too complex with ones mantra creation. One can just combine letters to do a mantra. One of the many books on runic energy that I read way back in the day suggested taking a consonant and then combing it with all the vowels in sequence. So the Feoh rune, being the letter "F" and therefore referring to material things such as food, nourishment, money, work, survival, careers and the like could be chanted like this "FA – FE – FI – FO – FU". Those who believe in such things would say that as you chant the mantra, the energy of the relevant rune will appear to you, I can't support that with the same level of certainty that they do, but I can say that a meditation with the letter F seems to have a different effect on the mind and body than when one uses the letter B as in the Beorc runic letter. Essentially there is a different "feeling" that is invoked, a different sensation. Be creative about these things and work out which one works well with your own subjective reactions to the sounds. I personally feel that if you were to use the "Ah" sound, you can probably do better at astral projection. But you don't need to chant "Ah" out loud. You can just sum it up in your own minds eye, what does it feel like when the "choir Ahs" sound? What feeling was the movie creator trying to sum up when the clouds scroll away to reveal a poetic vision of the afterlife and again you hear the "Ah" chanting? Something celestial, heavenly, something of the higher levels of being or some superior level spiritually speaking. This is the feeling that you need, it lifts you up. Calms you down and it a hymn in its on right.

Can you create it? Can you cultivate that in your mind "visualise" the sound and the feeling associated with the sound? If you can't then use the sound itself.

I have tried "Ah" meditation using a low frequency quite close to the lowest one that I can sing. It didn't give me that celestial meaning that I wanted to from the Ah sound. Spontaneous visualisations did come to me, but they were of caves, subterranean rivers and caverns. It was plain to me that the pitch of the note that I was using was too deep for me and I needed to use my Ah meditation at a higher frequency, but still one that was melodic and positive sounding. Once I increased the pitch of the note that I was using, I was capable of getting more interesting spontaneous visualisations of angelic beings flying between the planets. It was plain to me as a result of this experience that the pitch of the mantra has an impact on the resultant psychological effect.

Don't forget that meditation itself, the most simple of all metaphysical activities is powerful. Buddhists who dedicate their entire lives to compassion meditation show a dramatic change in brain structure to the point whereby two otherwise unconnected parts of their brain become fused. The Buddhists in question had created conditions whereby they could feel compassion with greater ease. You are attempting to use meditation to train yourself to become better at astral projection, so you need to work on meditation that helps with the sense of being outside of the body, a sense of otherworldliness of a spiritual nature and something that gives one the euphoric high frequency (gamma?) brain wave activity that some report as being the cause of supernatural experiences such as those that deal with spiritual activities. Thus you have to choose your mantra with great care and rearrange as many things as you can to make it happen.

Also when you are training yourself, think about your posture. You need to develop the astral spiritual state of mind using the Ah sound, but how are you going to increase the ability to make it happen? Visualising the "crown chackra" opening can be a very beneficial exercise. A beam of light coming from your head and reaching up to the sky or maybe a bolt of lightning coming down from the heavens and helping you to "open up" can be good, but make it even more spiritual seeming through turning the palms of your hands upwards so that you are reaching up to the sky in an almost worshipful way. It is true that religious people do this instinctively, but you can do this without being religious or spiritual by your nature. Just try it. It seems to be a good theatrical add-on that can help in the suspension of disbelief. Yes, I do believe that religious people may get more spiritual sensations and experiences, but they ascribe the experience to God, whereas I ascribe it to nature.

Incidentally, I have tried in the past, to use the concept of God to help me in reaching the state of mind for an astral projection. I chose the mantra "I am ascending slowly to reach God" and found it really rather powerful. Whether God exists is an irrelevance, the words had a degree of power to help me generate the experience.

When you are there, in that mediation, trying to have that kind of "Ah" spiritual sensation, try and push it to the limit. Feel the sense of gentle tranquil euphoria rising and rising in you to the point whereby it feels almost like you can't stand it anymore and then carry on, but let go as well. You are not trying to stress yourself out with this exercise, but you are trying to reach that state of euphoria, that state of mind that can be summed up as the state of mind that the designers of the most beautiful cathedrals in the world was trying to make you feel purely by the beauty of their architecture. You can push it to the limit, but not by tensing up your muscles or feeling the sense of motivation giving yourself indigestion. It has to be done in the mind alone and with a certain level of reverence for the religious state of mind that you are dealing with at this time in your explorations. Try and learn again to enjoy it. This giddying sensation many find difficult, but as I have pointed out, it is so important when it comes to leaving the physical behind, hitting that gamma brain wave frequency note and getting it just right with all the sensations in the mind's eye to help. It can be hit and miss, but it becomes more "hits" when you get used to it. It's kind of like the take-off point for a conscious projection experience and it is something that you need to get used to so that you can do it with greater ease when you are unconscious and asleep through the first stages to avoid the fear of getting outside of yourself in the first place. Practice may not make perfect, but it sure can make some success more likely.

At this point, learn to use it, make it work for you and allow the euphoria to do part of the work for you, start the visualisation of the rising sensation. You might fall prey to trying to concentrate on the two bodies at the same time as if you are wondering which one your consciousness will be in. Don't. Only think about the one body, the on body that you want to be in, the astral body. But as this is an exercise of visualisation, don't start to debate the existence of the things that you are visualising, but get on and do it. If you find it difficult to imagine a body made of light, appearing in a manner that is unaccustomed to you, then don't. Visualise the body that is familiar to you, the physical one, and visualise that one rising. You can visualise it as seen from outside if you wish, as if you were watching a movie of the experience, or you can try and be the experience itself. So long as the time of the visualisation remains constant. You, rising slowly, going up.

12

Take your time over this. It's not like you are in any hurry is it? No. Try and do this as if it were a work of art, a skill to improve, like a painting that you wanted to create, perfecting the small movements, taking time over it, doing it slowly and deliberately and with as much suspension of disbelief as you can muster up. Build up a sense of knowledge that the thing that you are visualising, your spirit body, is, for the purposes of this visualisation, the real you, it is you, you are "there" in some real sense of the word, build up that quality of identification with the spirit body and take it seriously enough to do it well, but not so seriously that yo want to enter an online debate about the objective existence of what you are visualising.

Keep that state of mind through the "Ah" state of mind with you as you go. Make it an exercise in enjoying a spiritual experience which you can have with or without a belief in the divine. Make mental notes as you go through the experience though, but spend less energy on that and more energy on the actual experience of the projection itself. Keep on going. You have nothing to fear and you make yourself enjoy the experience.

What happens after that point can be very variable. There can be snatches of visual effects, scenes, voices, pieces of music and strange lights. It does depend on what you are investigating as to whether you chose to pay attention to these things or not. If you are seeking the astral projection experience, it would be more beneficial to keep your attention on that and to not worry about the other phenomena that might or might not come to your senses. You will usually feel as though some parts of your body are out of the physical. Enjoy the experience. It's just strange and doesn't matter all that much until you get yourself deeper into the experience. A totally conscious projection is unlikely under these conditions, but it can happen, so if you don't get a totally conscious OOBE experience then practice the part meditation or pathworking type experiences and see how you go with that. I give some examples from my own experience further on in this essay of some mistakes that I have made in trying to perfect this art, it would be worth while checking that out and trying to avoid those mistakes. But as some of the sensations that you get in the experience start to follow the classic path of the astral body, work with that and practice improving the situation so that you can actually make the experience more and more like a "genuine" projection. Momentary glimpses of hat the material world looks like at various stages in your meditative experience should be classed as being a positive thing and you need to carry on working with that. Try and learn the mood when the happen. Once you have that mood, try and remember that mood when you are out projecting and see if you can bring about another "glimpse" of the real world as you are doing your pathworking exercise.

*

Here follows some personal experiences that I have had with the subject of astral projection. Try and study them well and use the information that is contained in them to your best advantage so that when you are out there and practising, you can try and base the experiences that you have during lucid dreams, during meditations and pathworkings on what I have written here.

My history with experiencing astral projections was long and really rather strange. When I was a child I visited my grandmother's (my father's mother) house with my sister. I am sure my mother and father needed some time together alone as parents often do, and so we spent the week with grandma. On one particular morning she was out at church and I was sat with my sister in the front room. We were doing the normal stuff that kids do, puzzle books, colouring in and the like, but I grew tired and bored and decided to try something new. I just sat down and started to imagine something. What it would be like to go through that wall over there? What would I see and what would it be like? I didn't actually know what was in the next room and so I saw this as a challenge (I am unsure why I got this idea in my head). So I half closed my eyes and imagined myself leaving my body and going for a short journey. For some reason I couldn't visualise myself walking across the living room floor and to the wall in question, so I had to visualise myself floating about 2 ft above the floor. I didn't detect any other presences around me, but I do recall that it almost seemed as though I was stationary and the rest of the house was moving around me to allow me to take the path in question. I put this down to the fact that the sensations of being seated on the upholstered sofa was too strong. But the visualisation carried on and I managed to get as far as the wall of the living room. Whilst I was there, I found it odd that I was struggling to get through the wall in the visualisation, and if this was just all in my head, just a daydream, then what was stopping me from getting through the wall? With some perseverance in the state of mind that I now know must have been meditative, I eventually got through and saw the dining room that we rarely used (as we did most of our eating in the kitchen that week). Once I was though I allowed myself to look around and see the position of the furniture, and then chose to return to my body and like any other child told my sister what I had done. She humoured me the way that any big sister could. But after that moment I had a look at the dining room and found to my surprise that the position of the chairs was just as I had "seen" it in the alleged daydream. It was curious. At that age and being as sceptical about my own experiences as many children were, I was dismissive about the experience until much later in life.

With what I know now I would have to say that I was probably doing a semi-conscious astral projection, not the full Monty, but a good quality semi-conscious projection. I have since learned to have fun with my semi-conscious projections, but not to trust them in their entirety as one's own preconceptions can get in the way of something meaningful being gleaned from the experience in question. However, I also have come to the hypothesis that younger people due to the differences in their brain chemistry and structure are much more prone to this kind of clairvoyant type activity. There have been many other incidents from my childhood whereby I seemed to gain knowledge by an apparently clairvoyant means that was not as a result of anything physical, but they aren't a relevant to the subject of astral projection and so they have to be left out of this essay. Still, this first experience was, as I have become known for saying, one of the many strange experiences to add to the collection.

My childhood itself was full of dreams that had aspects to them that connect with other people's reports of astral projections which makes me feel that there could have been an AP aspect to them. On one such a night I was fast asleep but playing with my Lego bricks on a cloud. The cloud itself was no cartoon cloud, but had all the same wispiness and cloud-like nature that all the low clouds that are capable of creating rain look like. In my dream I dropped a Lego brick and watched it fall down to the front garden of my house. I do find it strange that I had at that age (about three or four) such a well-developed mental image of what our house would have looked like from above for it to be just a dream me not having much access to television nor Ariel photographs at that time (late nineteen seventies). I dived after the Lego brick and fell through the sky having one of the most intense falling dreams that I could ever recall. I didn't wake up when I hit bottom, but the dream body came level with my bedroom window and I whipped through the closed window back to my sleeping body and awoke then with a gasp.

Another curious dream experience happened at about the time when I discovered the wonders of Saturday morning television. There were often some TV shows about flying characters. Reruns of Rocketman from the golden days of black and white science fiction cinema entertainment. Saturday picture show stuff. Also Superman. I got obsessed in my childhood days with the idea of flying and doing so just because I wanted to, by my own will and not by any other force of nature. I had at that time dreams about flying around my bedroom, but the curious thing about those dreams was that I would always notice a line that at times seemed to be golden and at times seemed to be silver that either trailed behind me or tugged me down to wake me up. Sometimes in the dream, it did seem to be drawn down to my bed. Was I seeing the Astral Cable in a very early astral projection? I still don't know. In one of these dreams I was hovering at ceiling height or just under it and could get a good view of what was on top of my wardrobe. This experience was curious as when my mother came up to tidy my room, the things I saw in my dream were the very same things that she pulled down from up there. A plastic sword, a hat, a bowl. It was very strange. I know these things happened such a long time ago, but I remember them as they left such an impression upon me. It was also at about this time in my life that I had my first ever ghost experience. But that story is for another essay. One thing that seems to be true here is that it was the obsession that I had for flying that enabled me to have this experience and that's what gave me the first idea that being obsessive about having a strange experience would be part of the way that these things can be made to happen, but maybe once the stress of the desire for the experience has been set in place, we then need to be somehow distracted away from them to release the subconscious mind's power to have the strange experience. Either that or a sufficient suspension of disbelief and total immersion in the idea to make it happen.

Moving home when I was just six years of age to our new location in south Buckinghamshire was both intensely exciting and pleasurable as well as very traumatic for me. On the first night when we as a family arrived at the new house, my mother made me butterscotch instant whip as a light but friendly dinner and I settled in for my first night in the new house. It was very strange for me and it just dawned on me that I was now many miles away from my school friends in London. I am not sure how it affected me but I sure did get many nights when I was not in my own (new) bedroom and I would fly sideways back to my bed before waking up. It was classic astral projection type dreams. Sometimes it was more like I was on my bed and my bed itself was moving, driving like a car or swaying around like a boat at anchor. Experiences that I eventually came to recognise as sleep projections, again of a semi-conscious type. Had my experiment at my grandmother's house trained me up to have these experiences? I will never know. Being exposed to new germs in the new area didn't do my health any good and I was frequently ill with many problems including a stomach ailment that eventually manifested itself as a form of post viral fatigue syndrome. My weakened heath condition gave me many more strange experiences. It's my firm opinion that in some stares of ill health one is more likely to get these strange experiences. So I was both disastrously unlucky to get ill, but incredibly lucky to have these experiences.

Occult activity from that time until my mid-teens seemed to slow down somewhat, but then things started to take off with vengeance. Some of the experiences that I have had I admit, could be put down to a B vitamin deficiency, but there are others that were harder to explain by any other means apparent from by something "supernatural". And, on top of that, it is possible that my B vitamin deficiency and other health issues may have had the effect of, in a drug free way, inducing the kind of shamanistic consciousness that can be required to make these strange things happen. I would frequently in my childhood for example, see spectral hands coming out of the floor, rising like waves and then falling again, often accompanied by a sighing noise as if some long dead person was turning over in their sleep. I just called them "the waving hands" and ignored them and assumed that other people had that experience too (after all, who doesn't consider themselves to be totally normal all the time?). As my diet improved and I was given B vitamins and minerals to help my with my fatigue, the waving hands experiences faded until they were just a memory. But another set of experiences happened that seemed to show me that not only was an astral projection possible, but that perception across not only space, but also time could occur too.

This was the era of the new found young and upwardly mobile class of people, the spirit of the nineteen eighties was in full force and there was a new middle class that was capable of moving away from mother and father at an earlier age. These people sought spirituality to help them in their success and to give them comfort. They used what was a basic form of occultism to help them to achieve this. Meditation of a Buddhist nature was popular. One day my mother told me about the chant that these new middle class used. Mainly for fun, but being young and earnest in my pursuit of life itself, I took it seriously and started to practice mantra meditation.

I started to practice the mantra every night for just ten minutes and schooled myself quite well in getting the mantra as good as I could get every night. I just did it quietly a I was rather self-conscious, and yes I did start to get some good benefits from it, but not quite enough for me to consider myself to be rocketing forward in terms of health. But the exercise did allow me to have some strange experiences that started to give me some more interest in the subject.

13

One night I decided to get myself to bed and my mind was full of the excitement f the new occult sciences that I believed that   had learned. I had at that time, through listening to silly people who had misinterpreted the writings of the traditional western occultists and considered magick to be a science, I focused my mind on the subject of astral projection. I tried to get to sleep, but to no avail, I had got myself so excited by the idea of wanting to project and how cool it would be, I had forgotten to try and deliberately relax. But eventually nature took over, and I slowly moved closer to sleep. My obsession had kept me on the edge of being awake as my body reached slowly into snooze mode. I was starting to have a lucid dream. Pulses of bluish colour moved across my vision as I lay there in bed partially in the curled up position of one who is sleeping. I started in my REM sleep to hear sounds, snatches of voices and also a feeling of there being presences around me. I hoped that I could use this state to launch myself in astral projection and started to think about "up". Seeing "rising" as a concept and trying to immerse myself in it. Then the most curious thing happened, I felt as though I was moving, but rotating slowly clockwise a few degrees and then anticlockwise, it was at a slow and steady rhythmic moving and then there seemed to be a turning of the axis of rotation and I was slowly moving from a swinging clockwise and anticlockwise movement, to a tilting upward position. It was very slow as if a hand was manually trying to move a heavy boat that was floating on a still pond. The movement grew more intense until I was head upright, but the body was still in the womb position, curled up on the bed, but upright. I was seeing strange things then, stalagmites and other rock formations, all glistening with a bluish yellow blow, but also somehow strangely black like pitch. The texture to the sense of being somehow changed and the visuals around me morphed into a blue mist, not the usual bluish yellow of the astral world, but that then passed and I found myself sitting bolt upright on my bed, cross legged. For some reason I was incapable of looking down to see my bed and body, but I was aware of being cross legged in bed (just as I know that my feed are crossed beneath me under this chair without me having to see them to know that that is the case). I was in the astral, and I knew that I was as the normal bluish yellow creamy light of the astral world was there. There were no shadows. But I was confused. I had no idea whether this was a dream or not. I looked forward to my door to see two elderly ladies there. Standing in the frame of the door in the place that would be illuminated by the light of the hallway had the light in the hallway been on and I was in a position to see it. I said something, I can't recall precisely what, but I was a young man with an attitude problem and it was probably something rather socially inappropriate, and it made the ladies laugh as if I was being too rude for words, the kind of "I beg your pardon!" kind of laugh, and I found myself being pushed so it seems, back into the physical body and I awoke with a good recollection of the entire experience. Something happened that night. Could those ladies have been my spirit guides or maybe spirits of the place, maybe people who had died and for some reason felt the need to stay there in the house because they felt attached to it? We will never know.

On another occasion, I had decided to stay up late for a period of many nights. I was trying to deliberately tire myself out so as to make astral projection attempts easier, and on top of that there was usually some fun, but poorly written and acted paranormal fiction on TV late at night. I was hoping to enhance my dedication to ghost stories to assist me in building up the obsession for the phenomena at hand. I had, for many months, been rehearsing in my mind's eye the whole route of the spirit body, from rising out of my body, gliding horizontally to the place there the astral cable wouldn't be able to control the body as much, then gliding down to the landing floor and then I was going to awaken in the astral and commence experiencing my projection. As I started to go to sleep, I automatically blacked out and lost consciousness completely, but just before the curtain of darkness came over me, I felt a "losing my stomach" kind of feeling the way that one does when going over a hump backed bridge in a car at speed, it was a kind of a yelping sensation, but it didn't disturb me for some reason and the darkness landed on me properly. I came too slowly, rather unsteady on my feet, saying a little as if I hadn't got my sea legs yet or that I was still marginally under the power of the astral cables pushing and pulling. I realised that my first mistake was to have chosen to materialise too close to my body for on that night for whatever reason, the power of the cable was stronger than on other nights and stronger than I had anticipated. But still I was there! I realised what had happened, and I took a few more steps towards my father's study so as to escape the pull of the cable and I got steady on my feet again. Everything was bathed in the usual astral light that I was getting used to. But now I was stuck. I was awake and fully conscious and it was the dead of the night an I hadn't planned a series of activities for me to do. I was alone and bored to a degree. Thus my second mistake was to not have a structured series of activities that I wanted to do, whether it was or something as simple as to go for a walk in the country or to visit a friend and communicate a message to them. As I lived in a terraced house at the time, I decided to try and walk through the wall into the house next door. I thought that this wouldn't be too hard as I had already projected through the closed door of my bedroom. I turned around and faced the wall and reached out my hands to touch or press against the wall and tried to us my passive willpower to move my body through the wall. The wall kind of felt as though it had a soft magnetic field around it as though my hands and the wall were two similar poles of a magnet, but the field was weakening, and I was able to start to push my hands through. Next I tried to get my head though and then I was hearing the sound of steam gushing from the wall itself as though the wall was of some porous material and my head was a gas of sorts and it had to pass through the wall like flour through a sieve. So my third mistake was to attempt to push myself through the wall rather than to attempt to appear on the other side of the wall at the twinkle of an eye. As I was attempting this task which felt strangely hard, I heard noise, my mother was getting up to go to the bathroom, an I suddenly elevated up to near ceiling height and went horizontal in the air and, head first, whooshed back to above the physical and then descended quickly back into the physical and awoke with a jolt. It was strange that the astral took a kind of an "S" shaped path to the physical going across the hallway to my closed bedroom door, through the closed door very quickly and then across the room to my bed. It was as though my mind couldn't allow my body to go back any other way apart from the route that it was familiar with during my waking and walking state, avoiding the stair well, but to do so up in the air and levitating.

On another occasion I had got it into my head that the Third Eye chackra was the most important one for bringing about the experience of an astral projection (naturally whether this is true or not is an irrelevance, but that region of the body does seem crop up a lot in mine and other peoples reported experiences). The colour that was associated with that part of the body was supposed to be purple. So I entered a transcendental meditation trance and attempted to meditate on that colour. To be able to visualise it as if I was engulfed in it, as if the whole of my aura (kind of like an egg shaped ball of energy around my body) was of that colour, a beautiful purple plasma that moved and flickered in a similar manner to the plasma energy in a plasma ball lamp around the emitter. I tried to fill my mind with it whilst I was in seated meditation. I tried to sum that state of mind up, as if purple was a state of mind. I tried to "feel purple" if such a thing exists! And to associate all of this with the third eye chackra region in the forehead just above the middle of the eyebrows. That night I tried to do an astral projection to see a friend of mine. When I met him the next day I asked him what he dreamed of, and he said "actually I dreamed of you but I dreamed that you were wearing an allover purple suit".

One night in my teens I had a very vivid projection. I went to bed at my normal time and wasn't thinking about anything spiritual, occult or religious to the best of my recollection. I was exceptionally tired. I was lying on my bed and was sure that I was not getting to sleep. I had been struck with insomnia. I felt pretty alert, but I was still very tired. I decided to resign myself to the fact that the body didn't want to physically move despite the fact that I wanted to get up and do something constructive in my apparent insomnia. I decided to carry on resting, lying comfortably the way that a person does as they try and get to sleep. I have no idea how long I lay there, but after a time I felt that I was moving, as if I was on an air bed floating on a rippling stream. Swaying this way and that as if I was a boat at anchor and not quite being capable of controlling the movements as I pivoted about my head and rested on the slow and gentle undulating waves. I was unsure as to whether I felt comfortable about this and tried to move my resting body, but I found that I could not. It seemed that I was in a kind of sleep paralysis state, but I was still awake, or conscious. Before my eyes, colours started to move across my vision, blues and greens and yellows, again in waves, sometimes concentric circles, sometimes zigzags. Unfortunately I still couldn't move my physical body at all and again I felt as awake as I do now. It seems that at the point when I resigned myself completely to the experience and decided that there was nothing that I could do about this apart from to enjoy it, that the sensations changed and instead of the swaying like a boat at harbour and being on a bed of undulating waves, I started to move upwards, as if the container that I was in was being filled up with more water and I started to rise. The sensations of the waves became more intense and it was couples with a kind of a spiritual euphoria, tranquil, but still euphoric. The funny colours that I was seeing increases in their rate and started to blur into a new singular colour, the astral bluish yellow cream mistiness! I was having a spontaneous astral projection! I could feel myself moving upwards at a slow and steady rate, it was coupled with a kind of a buzzing noise like or similar to the fifty hertz buzz of an amplifier that is connected to the mains electricity. The buzzing noise seemed to come and go and when it was strongest that was when he astral body seemed to rise more or with more purpose and when it faded the astral slowed down or stopped ascending all together. It was as if the buzz itself was the sound of the engine that was making the astral body move. The sound of the subconscious will exerting itself on the movement of the spirit body. The mistiness in my vision started to clear and then I saw my bedroom from the position of the astral body just a few feet above the bed that I was physically lying on and all in the colours of the astral body's world. I got a sense of vertigo, which, contrary to my normal modus operandi, didn't give me fear, but instead seemed to be turned into a willingness to project further. It's hard to describe the way that the mind can turn vertigo in to something that can be useful, it kind of transforms the feeling into pleasure, as if you were learning how to masochistically enjoy something that you had previously hated. I ascended further until I was nearer the ceiling and then I started to slide as if being pulled, out of my own control and even against my will, by my feet. It was alarming to feel that far out of control, but the sensation of sliding was similar to the sensation of sledging down a hill with new snow. I slowed down in speed as the astral (still with me paralysed and not having any real ability to do anything about what I was experiencing) when I reached the top of the stairs where I righted in the same manner as usual. I was in a different bedroom at this time of my life and the stairs were nearer my bed. This would explain the fact that I was still affected by the astral cable or so it seems. I was swaying, standing upright, but pivoting on my feet slowly as one might if one was restrained by guide-ropes that were made of elastic. However, throughout the whole experience, my body, my spirit body was still in the same position and posture that it was in in the bed. Half curled up, one arm over my head. I was totally paralyzed throughout the experience. It was very strange.

After having studied the Malleus and having read the stories that were in it, the way that the witches of old attempted to explore the astral world, I decided for the first time to give it a try. I designed a creative visualisation that was in a similar manner to a pathworking exercise, but I didn't do it with any sense of changing my surroundings, it was more of a self-guided meditation. I still using visualisation and with the same quality that I have spoken of already in this essay. I chose to visualise my body from the outside, but also to attempt this from an "Ah" meditation state of mind. Namely reaching some kind of tranquil spiritual mood prior to actually doing the exercise itself. I imagined that I was seated in a chair passively watching my resting body on the bed and watching me attempt the astral projection exercise. I watched and visualised the blue plasma like a liked of airborne snot or a vapour or smoke of a bluish hue slowly exiting from the nostrils of my resting body. The blue smoky plasma started of like a small ball and then extended itself a tendril, a snakelike wisp of vapour which could extend infinitely. I tried to tell myself that what I was doing was watching the real self, the spirit itself slowly leaving the body as I watched that tendril of plasma exiting the nostrils of the body. It was kind of like feeling a sense of something exiting from my lungs, the breath of life itself, being transferred to the blue misty plasma smoke. My physical body started to feel less full of life somehow as I watched that plasma move and extend to a free area of my bedroom to the side of my sleeping body where it started to collect like water running off and collecting in a puddle, but a three dimensional puddle that was oval in shape, standing on its end and roughly the height of a human being, me to be exact. I tried to visualise this as clearly as I could and to make the visualisation as powerful and real as I could, including down to the wisp that connected the physical body's nose and the head area of the newly visualised astral body. Now for the hard part! Trying to form that oval of mist into the shape of my own body. I worked hard at it taking into account al the time when I had studied my own from, my posture, my face, my body and limbs. At that time, I curious thing happened. Remember I was visualising this from the position of outside of my own body and as if I was seated in a char beside my own bed whilst I was visualising this happening. I found it hard to keep my position in the imaginary chair. It was as though I was being sucked in to the new form that I was building for myself. My sense of self and consciousness was no longer happy being away from either my physical body or my imagined spiritual body. After a time (that I was incapable of measuring), something "snapped" and I was no longer capable of sitting in the chair. I was whipped up and in a moment of whooshing through the air I was in the astral and standing in the location that I was visualising the body being in. It was not a totally conscious projection, but it was a projection none the less and although it seemed rather dreamlike, the movements of the body were in agreement with the movements (pivoting on the feet) of an astral projection. I felt at that time that I could go anywhere in the world. It was a kind of a successful attempt to create an experience as I did actually get the symptoms of the experience I was working towards, but I did miss out on creating the fully conscious projection. It was probably the kind of state that one may need to be in if one wants to share dreams with other people or to attempt apparent spirit contact.

14

Sometimes one gets an experience that makes one feel that there are more things that can bring about the resultant astral projection or remote viewing experience. Have you ever look at yourself from another perspective? And I don't mean allegorically or introspectively! I am not sure what was wrong with me at that particular time of my life. I do recall having some dizzy spells and some symptoms of a cold, but nothing to extreme. Or maybe it was all down to something that I ate? I don't really know, but I was queuing at the bank, rather irritated that I had a problem to solve that was not really any of my fault. We have all had moments like this. And I got one of those moments of dizziness, but I was able to stand my ground. I didn't fell down and I do recall holding on to the rail that we all had to queue beside whilst waiting for the cashiers to be free. A moment of calm came upon me and I was actually looking down for a brief second, on to the top of my own head. This was disconcerting as it made me aware that I had not brushed my hair this morning and that I looked rather poor quality and started to wonder what other people felt about someone who was this scruffy. But, the experience lasted for just a few seconds. It's like I faded into it and then faded out of it and then ended up back into my body and was capable of continuing with the rest of my chores. The experience stayed with me all day long. Was it the fact that I was feverish that lowered my sensitivity to the astral, was the astral leaving the physical for a moment to get some nourishment or was I just blacking out to allow the body to do some kind of necessary neutralisation of toxins in the system and the experience was purely down to hallucination? Its hard to say, but one thing that did strike me as odd is that when I went back home, feeling self-conscious about my hair, I used a combination of mirrors to view he top of my head and the back and saw that yes, my hair really did look like that from behind. The vision that I saw was in fact accurate and it showed me something about myself that I seemed otherwise oblivious to. Why the body and mind would do this to me I still don't know.

Sometimes attempts at astral projection can overlap with apparent ghost experiences. In my twenties I was kind of going to a certain bar where they held banquets and on one particular occasion I stayed the night after a session of music and dining. I wasn't a drinker in those days (I was teetotal) and I didn't take any drugs. At about three o'clock in the morning when the party had slowed to a halt and everyone was going back to their rooms or was preparing to get some night sleep in their car, I unfurled my sleeping bag and set down to get some kip on the floor. It was early in the year, but it wasn't cold. It was hard to sleep on the flagstones in the pub beside the pool table, so I set about doing some kind of meditation. As the pub was very pagan friendly, I decided that a meditation based on the theme of the four elements as used in Wicca would be most appropriate. So I silently chanted the four elements in sequence the way that one does when doing a circle casting and used the relaxed state of mind to attempt to bring abut an astral projection. I started to visualise my body ascending and moving towards the ceiling. I was, so it seemed rather unsuccessful at doing the projection itself, but I again had another kind of strange blackout that seemed to give some kind of spiritual visualisation. I felt someone approaching very rapidly, as if they were aware that I was doing something interesting and wanted to find out what I was up to, and, for a few seconds, I was again in the astral colour vision of blue and yellow cream light and a child, maybe about ten years of age was standing over my body. He had piercing blue eyes and wavy wild black hair. For some reason I wasn't surprised by the visitation and the child in question didn't seem to mean any malice to me, he just seemed to be curious as to what I was up to. Then he vanished and so did the astral colours and I was left in wonderment about what I had seen. I didn't get that much more sleep that night due to excitement about the experience.

Going to university with all of the trials and tribulations of student life was a great time to do some practice in astral projection. By this time I was heavily interested in means of altering the state of consciousness without drugs, but still using artificial means. I had bought myself a basic mind machine (a strobe light device that exerts an influence on the brain waves whilst you are in meditation) and used that as a basic tool to help me to do some astral projections. It was a basic machine with only four programs (this was very early in the history of the mind machine market), but it still did the job. The complex layout of the very modern university that I was studying in was confusing to me, being a young man who hadn't really got his "system sorted out" as of yet. That sense of confusion combined with the usual post-adolescent anxieties probably heightened my state of awareness to a degree, and even to the point of paranoia at times, but that was ok (for the purposes of experimenting with astral projection at least!). It was a great little mind machine and I would often use the stimulation program prior to going to the dance hall, the night club and sometimes even out to the student bar. But, between some lectures and classes, if I was tired or stressed, I would retire to use the mind machine. Staying up late, eating a bad diet and generally not looking after myself was great when it came to projecting. Many of my attempts were only half projections, I would get the sensation of my feet, legs and lower body going up, and leaving the body, but I was at an angle with my head still connected to the physical. It was as though I was being lifted out by my feet and not allowed to go further. It was plain that being overtired and not doing too well physically could help create some sensations, but not all of the ones that I needed. The mistake that I had made here was that I needed to keep the mind fresh and clear, to use concentration and use it well, and mind machine or not. This requires looking after ones diet (which one can't do on un-nourishing supermarket "value" bread at a few pennies a loaf, and to which I seemed to be allergic anyway), one's nutrition (I hadn't bought multivitamins for a long long time), exercise (tried the gym and didn't get on with it, or so I told myself!) and sleep (at that time I was under the delusion that students weren't meant to do much of that). So being seriously run down, I couldn't exercise the quality of control that I needed to to make the experience work. That, however, didn't stop me from trying. I would frequently have dreams that had some kind of astral projection component to them. Flying dreams, dreams of walking around a stately home that had a similar layout to the university campus itself which could have been the astral going for a wander and trying to get used to the unfamiliar grounds. Many of my projection dreams were however a little more run of the mill, dreaming that I was a kite on the end of a long string and was being buffeted by the wind happened quite a lot. Probably an astral cable type dream.

However in one experience I was very conscious of being out of the body and walking around the grounds of the college. I saw someone walk my way, someone I was familiar with and who was going through some bad experiences at that time. He ignored me (presumably because I was or seemed to be in the spirit body) and walked straight through me. The shock of it sent me straight back to he physical body in a rushing of astral wind. The same person arrived at my door about thirty minutes later wanting to talk about some difficulties he had with some fellow students.

Many of my projection experiences in college centred upon the library. I probably spent more time in the library when out of the body then I did when in the body, or so it seems. I do recall a time when I was actually searching the shelves of the library to see whether a particular book that I needed was actually present there. I was doing this in the astral body. The information that I gained seemed to be totally accurate down to the books that were either side of the one that I wanted and even the dewey decimal number of the shelf area that I needed. But unfortunately, despite the intelligence that one is supposed to have when one enters university I didn't have enough intelligence to realise that this was probably a one off and I wouldn't necessarily be able to control the experience. Basically, I believed in the power of this phenomena to the point of believing that I had a power and one that was under complete conscious control and didn't put it to the test to explore the limitations of this phenomena. I attempted in meditation on countless other occasions to search the shelves of the library and often found myself to be wrong. Remote viewing can happen, but it is never the most controllable phenomena in the world. Sometimes it seems to happen when it wants to or when the subconscious willpower is so strong that it pulls the astral out when one has achieved a state of not thinking about such things. Other times it occurs like a semi-conscious astral projection and the mind fills in the blanks of detail with anything, and one mistakes the things that one sees with reality. Sometimes the mind fills in the blanks with things that used to be there long before you ever went near that place.

I wanted to experiment with astral projection and to see if it could have a life changing effect upon another human being at a distance. In my first year of university, I know this fellow student who was evidently more intelligent then me, but was drinking very heavily and not putting any time to get any studies done. I thought I would try and project to him and to literally shake some sense into him. So on one night when the compulsory insomnia that many students have had set in I decided that I would use a combination of techniques, astral projection and pathworking and I would create a dream reality with him in it. Make it familiar to him and use that as a means of giving him a message that would change him and transform him. The I chose the all too familiar licensed dance hall that was in the basement of the college and chose to "meet" him there and to grab him by the collar and then to shout at him that he should work harder. I performed the astral experience and didn't tell him or anyone that I had done it. After about three quarters of a year, I went on a pub crawl with him at Christmas and as we were setting into the second or third round of drinks the subject of mad dreams came up. He suddenly explained "I had this really weird dream about nine months ago. I dreamed that Nick met me in the dance hall and grabbed me by the collar and shouted 'you must work harder, you must work harder' at me!" So the experiment was a success to a degree, but unfortunately that student dropped out of college and after a few more drinking sessions I didn't hear from him again. Can astral projection be used to change lives at a distance? I don't know, but I can say that I have had a series of experiences that have changed mine.

After university I was, just like many young and rebellious men, wanting to get away from my parent and from that time there came a string of jobs that were poorly chosen for me and didn't take into account my needs nor a fair assessment of my character nor what I wanted to actually do with my life. Quite a common pattern in the lives of many young men. This pattern of behaviour lead me to move my address quite a lot as a result of this. That seemed to create a certain degree of disorientation and dreams occurred in which I was not in the place of residence that I was staying. Sometimes I could put this down to nostalgia, or just a sense of displacement, but at other times the sense of being in the other location was so strong that it was almost impossible for me to think that I was not there in some manner.

The most interesting part of this was when the astral would travel back to the physical at the moment of waking the physical form. The body may be woken up by some noise in that area. I would get a sense of seeing from two sets of eyes simultaneously. The first being the physical body and seeing the room in which I was resting. The second being the eyes of the apparent astral body as it whipped at lightning speed across roads, through villages, past or over cars and peoples gardens, all of it being a blur and only the occasional small detail here and there being clear and describable. It was exciting. Thus it leads me to assume that maybe there was an aspect of astral projection to those dreams and the astral body was really travelling back to the physical body at speed to allow me to do my waking day.

The actual dreams themselves were quite boring. But what I saw was often curious. On one occasion I had moved out of my flat at night on Friday to move into a new flat the very same night. My normal routine had been disrupted and I found myself sleeping in a strange bed. As the experience of moving home yet again was distressing I wanted to get an early night and went to bed as soon as I could. My nocturnal visions included seeing the landlord vacuum cleaning the room where I had previously been staying. The dream itself was calm, emotionally dispassionate, objective. I was observing him from a viewpoint that seemed to be hovering some two or three feet from the floor of the room and in the doorway. As if my "head" with its organs of sensory perception (stereoscopic 3D vision, hearing) was suspended on a fluid like tentacle the end of which was poking its head around the half opened doorway of the room in question. As with many experiences of this type, it was in the astral colours, or something similar to them. The fact that the colours were slightly "off" showed me that this was only partially conscious, so I can't be totally convinced of the objective validity of what I was seeing. Was I really projected and seeing the landlord cleaning the room? It certainly seemed that way. I watched all the details of setting up the vacuum cleaner, using his foot to activate the mains cable release, uncoiling the mains cable and plugging the plug into the familiar socket that previously powered my bedside light. All the details were right even down to the scuff marks on the mains socket, the frayed ends of the rug, the red curtain that was too short with its missing curtain hook on one end. Apart from the odd position of the movement and position of my head and the strange bluish yellow colours of the astral experience it was as though I was there for a few minutes spying on him. I was again, just as conscious and awake as I am right this very minute and typing up this essay. If we are to be honest we must also not discount the possibility that I was dreaming and that my mind was filling in the gaps. But it was so detailed and was so similar to other experienced that I have had that appeared to be genuine projections or had all the characteristics of a good and genuine experience, that it seemed then (and still does seem) unlikely that it was purely a dream. But I can only base this on the quality of the personal experience, I can't base that on anything else (for what else have I to go on?). I had half a mind to telephone the landlord and tell him what I had seen him doing, but as is often the case with ex landlords, I hadn't really got on well with him and had decided not to make contact and let it go.

15

I used to be a member of an eighteen to thirty club which at that time of my life I rather enjoyed. However, there was an Easter trip that was organised that turned rather sour. As one could expect in an environment where there are many young men who are full of the boisterous behaviour of young men, sometimes the behaviour would get out of hand. I had driven there in my parents car, and I wanted to look after it. I had parked it not too far away, but out of earshot.

I get my head to rest in the caravan in the afternoon in order to get enough energy to stay up and dance the night away, and decided to use the mind machine to help me to get off to sleep, or if I couldn't do that, then to meditate and recoup my energy that way. This I did with a degree of success, but as I was drifting into meditation accompanied by the flashing of the LED lights in the mind machine, I started to have a spontaneous experience of a most bizarre nature. I started to project. I felt my body move upwards in the traditional method that I have already mentioned earlier in this essay and to right itself just above my bed, but standing there in the same room of the caravan with me was another person. This person was not anyone that I recognised and they seemed to be rather old and with a gaunt and seriously age withered face of a nature that was so severe that it could be a character from a horror movie. I was shocked, but this person seemed to have a kindly if somewhat paranoid nature. I am unsure now as to whether this was a male or a female character. But it said "I detect a frightening male presence" and I immediately snapped out of the dream.

I got up and discounted the experience as just a dream until I left the caravan and found that the car has its tires let down and the car had been vandalised. At that point I connected the vision and what had happened to the car as some kind of warning that there were unbalanced people nearby and I acted to move the car off the premises as soon as I had pumped up the tires, repaired the damage as best I could and found some time.

Does this prove astral projection? No, but it does show that sometimes a person who practices astral projection exercises can at times have strange experiences. Does it prove the existence of spirit guides or angels? No, but it does show that under some circumstances that one can in a dream have something that appears to be a warning. Was I being warned? It is hard to say as one cannot state whether there was a causal link between the car being vandalised and the vision that I had experienced. But it sure as hell was curious.

Nick Dutch

Some people in the new age world speak of "shape shifting". Sometimes they say that this is to turn the astral body into the shape of an animal as a result of creative visualisation once one is projected. Some of these type of people study horror films, principally those connected with the werewolf mythology, but some connected to vampire stories, for the purposes of attempting to gain some kind of inspiration as to what it looks like for a person to turn from one creature (human) into an animal (wolf, bat etc.), I wanted to attempt such an experiment for myself and I set about following a similar methodology. I started watching numerous horror based TV shows and movies. The process would have seemed more interesting if I was more capable of entering into a fantasy world of the order and type that the creators of the movies and shows were trying to demonstrate. But unfortunately I was not able to achieve that particular state of mind straight away. Also there was another problem and that was when I was trying to enter into such states of mind using in depth creative visualisations, emotions which are traditionally considered to be negative to projection would be arisen, those of fear and anxiety. I discovered with perseverance that it was only when I had some malice against someone and I was in a deep state of anger and with violent emotions that the visualisations (myself into aggressor, wolf or bat, and them into submissive victim) was more achievable. This lead me to believe that the people who mainly had an interest in this particular exercise probably had something wrong with them, possibly a megalomania, a psychotic or sociopathic temperament. Definitely pathogenic and moving towards mentally unbalanced and socially undesirable.

No, I don't "believe" that all religious imagery is acceptable, nor that all spiritual creatures are acceptable in one's own psychological space. Sometimes meditating too hard on characters that are negative, whether they be fictitious or otherwise, can actually damage and unbalance your mind. The ideas an images that you put into your mind (which is what you do with occultism) is something that you need to take extreme responsibility for and taking responsibility for these things can be one of the most important activities that you do with your life. You have to keep yourself sane and the maintenance of a healthy balance of psychological ideas and imagery, especially those that lead to a healthy mind, are important as one goes through one's life.

But in the name of experimental occultism, I still decided to give the exercise a go. Using the word LUPUS LUNAR LYCANTROPE - LUPUS LUNAR LYCANTROPY as the basis of the mantra I started to do meditation. I made sure that I did this on the night of the full moon (to give the exercise atmosphere) and near the festival of Halloween. I had given my mind a good diet of some of the more chilling werewolf imagery that I could find, including watching a certain well known movie which features the image of a man turning into a wolf as part of its special effects. On to of that I had watched a few documentaries on the subject of wolf and had a good idea of the howl of the creature and some basic pack behaviour. I had pretty much studied enough of the modern mythology of supernatural lycantropy as one possibly could.

The time of day was near midnight and I was doing this exercise prior to preparing for bed to make sure that my dreams were full to the maximum that night of wolfish nightmarishness.

I started the meditation nice and slowly, focusing my mind on the shape and forms of a wolf as best as I could. I was chanting out loud, nice and quiet, but still out loud. I kept my eyes half closed as I tried to build up the imagery in my mind's eye. I could feel myself entering into the focused state of mind that I was used to feeling on my mind machine session (probably the best psychic training exercises I have ever done were on a mind machine) and I could make the experience of filling my mind with wolfiness more and more powerful.

Although I was definitely more capable of "invoking" something of the wolf into my mind and being during the meditation session itself, nothing much happened in the meditation and I found myself unable to do sufficient astral projection activity, possibly due to the fear that was brought about by focusing my mind on something that I myself was afraid of.

I went to bed slightly disappointed about he apparent failure of the meditation, but as I feel asleep something strange happened. Firstly I fell into a powerful and lucid dream, of a similar order of clarity as the "kundalini" dream that I have already mentioned. But this one was totally absent of all other characters and it was just me, lying on my back in a woodland glade at night, my body resting on a pile of rotting leave and with the scent, the most powerful scent, of woodland around me. I was in agony and my entire body was sore, it felt like I was about to break every fibre and cell in my body. I heard the words "The Curse of the Wolf!" being screamed at me, but the sound seemed to be from a female voice and also seemed to be coming from inside me. I screamed n fear and yes, my body in my dream turned into that of a wolf. It felt different. Everything about my body felt dog like, the shape of the rib cage, the shape and moveability of my legs. Even the hair the belly and genitalia area seemed to be canine like, but the hair was a kind of greyish colour and not the black of any nightmare wolf that I could dream of. Even my snout was dog like and in my field of vision. It was a terrifying experience. What was added to the experience and made it even more frightening, was a change in the state of mind that I had. I no longer felt human, I felt the need to hunt and kill, I wanted blood and hungered for it the way that a thirsty man hungers for water or the way a starving man longs to steal food. I had become for a moment the nightmare. The part of me that was human was horrified by the very real blood lust that I was under and wanted to return to being human again. This dream was so lucid it was impossible to separate it from that of any waking moment that I have had in good health of body and mind, which is what made the experience even more frightening in every possible way. But it seemed that the moment of terror was coupled by an ability to become human again and to wake up in the physical body sweating more than I have ever done after any nightmare.

After I had calmed myself down and tried to convince myself that it was only a dream and I had finally become quite normal and objective again, I returned to bed to try and finish off my night sleep. The next bout of dreaming was quite pleasant in experience and sensation. It "felt" like, or had the same emotional feeling as a regular projection sensation that one has when one is moving at intermediate speed from one location to another. I was moving forward through countryside. It was again a woodland setting, maybe familiar to me as I was at that time living in an area that was rich in managed woodland. But it was dominated by the same astral colours that had become familiar to me by then. I did not recall leaving the body and didn't recall arriving at the woodland in this particular experience. The thing that was strange about it was that I seemed to be bounding along. I wasn't running with my head at normal human height, it felt as though I was on all fours and bounding as a dog does when chasing a hare and with the speed and agility that one would expect a predator to be running at. But despite the rapid action of the body and the rapid movement from side to side as I swerved to avoid trees, bushes and the like, it was still a tranquil experience. It was as if the subconscious mind was taking over and moving the astral for me and I could just sit back inside the eyes of the wolf and watch the experience go by. The wolf spirit body stopped and looked up at the full moon and let out a sound that I heard and seemed to feel through my body. It was a wolf howl. At that moment, I felt myself being rushed back to the physical body and changing form as I did so to coincide with the physical from and I woke from the experience.

Had I actually projected out of the body and into the form of a wolf? Was I a spiritual werewolf? As is usual, I have to ask you how I am to test that that experience was what it seemed to be? Sure all the characteristics were there in the second dream experience for it to be an astral projection, but as I am wonderfully unaware of any stories of spectral wolves being seen at that time of year in the local woodland and I have not had the chance to survey the entire local town so as to evaluate what everyone had dreamed of that night I can't answer that question. As far as repeatability is concerned, I have only attempt to repeat the experience on a few occasions and not many of them primarily because the transformation dream was so inhuman and so unpleasant that it seemed unwise to repeat it. I don't see the point in going insane for science and neither should you!

16

In conclusion what can I say? Well, from the outset, my own personal experiences show and prove to me that a certain kind of personal experience (which under some strange circumstances and somewhat unreliably, seems to be transmittable to others) can occur. It seems to follow the same lines as that which is described by our culture as an astral projection or out of body experience and can be brought about deliberately, to a degree, with the help of a series of creative visualisations and changing ones focus of attention as to where a person is, a certain disassociation away from the physical body, dizziness and the like. It seems to occur more when one is ill or over tired on the basis that one can maintain ones awareness (consciousness) deep into a state of physical paralyses or something similar to that. It can, under some circumstances, provide you with what appears to be knowledge of things that are outside of your knowledge and things that are outside of your range of perception. Some rare experiences of this type can provide you with experiences of what appears to be otherworldly beings, spirits, ghosts, angels and the like. It can happen sometimes when one is awake if one gets dizzy spells for whatever reason, and can even occur if one's pattern of life is disrupted for instance, by moving house. It becomes more likely when one is obsessing about the phenomena in question and one has a good fantasy life that is dominated by the nature of the experience. It also becomes easier if one becomes a skilled mediator and has a good conceptualisation of one's self-image. It probably occurs with those who practice religious type exercises more (which, by their nature, are meditative and contemplative by nature) and therefore it is more likely that religious people will have such experiences or something similar to them.

It is an experience, and one that is for want of a better word, real. It occurs. But what it means we can never and will never be able to say (so far). It has become the foundation of many a new age religion and has been seen my some people as a corroboration of many different religious points of view, but that is the realm of belief and faith and as such has to be discredited if the movements associated with experimental occultism (the experiential experimental research into abnormal consciousness based phenomena) is ever to be taken seriously.

Despite having had many experiences with forms of astral projection, many more then I have written about here in this essay, and many experiences of a seriously abnormal nature, some of which have had an effect on other people, or seemed to, I cannot, by intelligence and reasoning, say that they give me an unquestioning faith in life after death, nor can I say that they assure me that there is a God, nor can I say that they are objective proof of the existence even of the astral body upon which I have been experimenting, let alone angels, spirits or ghosts.

The new age movement which many people adore, in practice isn't new. It's the rehashing of cult creation using the benefits of the broad distribution technology of the twentieth and twenty first centuries. In many cases it is the movement towards pre industrial pre scientific superstition and a form of religious literalism that is dominated by fear of supernatural beings. It has distorted even the writings of the classic occultists. The classic occultists that they consider to be their spiritual and moral guides. They have done this for the purposes of gaining power over others, earning money through intellectually immoral means, brainwashing people and extorting money as a result of weakening individuals the point of making them vulnerable through forms of religious bullying. All of this at the expense of research into nature.

Nature is the most important thing that we have. Through its study, we as a species have learned to fly, communicate over distances using telecommunications, and have eradicated many of the diseases that has in the past held our population down. Also we have walked on the moon, sent probes to the outer reaches of the solar system and have even used satellites to help us forecast weather and measure climate change. We as a species have harnessed forms of energy that otherwise we would not be able to use and used them as a mechanism to drive forward scientific progress. The study of nature has given us everything.

But, the movement that promises so much in terms of consciousness science, including such a basic thing as self-knowledge through introspection, the new age movement, has done more to destroy both mundane science and also consciousness research through the perpetual creation of new religions and cults. It has even distorted beyond that which is practical and rational, the study of the phenomena that is used as the basis and foundation of their movement, the apparently paranormal.

What does the new age movement promise? Too much. What does it deliver? Too little. How can that be changed? By changing the culture of the movement to being one that is driven by reason and rationality and away from religious warfare between competing groups, belief and superstition. That means a radical shift in the direction of the whole movement on a worldwide basis. Don't get me wrong, the phenomena that are written of in this essay, and so many more, are real natural phenomena. I have had them, and more. I am of the opinion that they are in the hands of anyone who has the capacity to dedicate themselves to have these experiences, but one cannot say at all that they are proof of any faith. They raise questions, but can't provide any answers, the only answer that can be provided is that they exist as experiences that can happen.

Why do we as a species busy ourselves with religious argumentation when we already know that religious argumentation is argumentation in a circle? Maybe it's a stage of life thing, helping children or some infantile grown-ups to grow up, but when we come face to face with a series of experiences that seem to defy everything that we know about the human animal and the way that we are put together, a greater importance looms in front of us like a massive library of wisdom stretching on as far as the horizon. A library of wisdom that has never before been studied by humankind. The greater importance is to stop worry about whether we are following the right religion and to stop wasting our time online arguing about whether our spiritual path is bigger and better than theirs. And as far as the creationism debate is concerned, give me air! These things are an irrelevance when we have our first ever conscious astral projection. We wonder whether we are spirit or whether we are flesh. We wonder whether our influence stretches beyond our body or not and we wonder whether this technology can be used to help heal the sick, to improve physical and mental health, to help us as a species to communicate over distance at zero cost. On top of that we wonder whether we can learn of a method to use occult exercises to help us to overcome psychological issues and therefore to cure psychological and possibly psychiatric health issues. We don't know how to control these forces (if they be forces at all), but some strange experiences show us *something*, but as of yet we still have too many questions and not enough answers.

We move closer to finding the answers when we stop putting a blurry object in between us and he search for the truth, that blurry object is religion, spirit based faiths and cult mentalities. The more religions we develop, the closer we get to dusk and the further away we get from the clear blue skies and piercing radiant Sun of the Truth of whatever is true.

Does an astral projection prove certain writings of Paul in the books of Corinthians? Who cares? We have a phenomenon. It happens in nature like birth. Let us stop worrying about what it means and make the phenomena a study in its own right. We may have to reach it though unempirical means, and we may have to practice some religious exercises or something similar to that to help us get the experience, but we don't have to join any religion at all no matter what anyone says.

Other Books of the Paramormal From WheelMan Press:

One of the biggest questions we have is "What happens when we die?" No one really knows except those who have already passed on. This book contains stories from nurses, doctors, and hospital staff who have witnessed death first hand. Some of the stories are beautiful, while others are terrifying.

Print: http://wlmpr.us/ASftERp
Kindle: http://wlmpr.us/ASftERk

Here are more stories from the ER, recountings from people who truly believe that they have had encounters with the world they believe is waiting for us beyond the grave. We hope that you find them as entertaining and awe-inspiring as before. Read them with an open mind and let your conclusions be your own.

Print: http://wlmpr.us/A2MSftERp
Kindle: http://wlmpr.us/A2MSftERk

What are Angels? By definition they are mythical beings, depicted as messengers of God in the Hebrew and Christian Bibles, along with the Quran. This book is a collection of stories about Angels and individual accounts of people who have had personal interactions with them. My hope is that through these stories you find comfort, and that you realize that no matter how bad things may seem, that you are never alone.

Print: http://wlmpr.us/ASHfABp
Kindle: http://wlmpr.us/ASHfABe

Spirit Walking: True Tales of Out of Body Experiences by Everett Stone, is just one of the terms used to describe the experience of having your spirit detach from your body and "walk" free for a brief time. There are both spiritual and scientific theories on the out-of-body experience, and controversy always follows this subject, many doubting the true existence of these types of phenomenon, while others base their entire world and spiritual views on these very sorts of things.

Print: http://wlmpr.us/SWOBEp
Kindle: http://wlmpr.us/ASHfABe

www.ingramcontent.com/pod-product-compliance
Lightning Source LLC
Chambersburg PA
CBHW031513040426
42445CB00009B/211